The Wisdom of Elizabeth Towne

GW00480710

Life Power and How to Use It
Just How To Wake The Solar Plexus
Happiness and Marriage

Wilder Publications, LLC.
PO Box 3005
Radford VA 24143-3005

ISBN 10: 1-934451-73-8
ISBN 13: 978-1-934451-73-1

First Edition

10 9 8 7 6 5 4 3 2 1

Life Power and How to Use It

Table of Contents:

Chapter I: Methuselah and the Sun

To see the beauty of the world, and hear
The rising harmony of growth, whose shade
Of undertone is harmonized decay;
To know that love is life—that blood is one
And rushes to the union—that the heart
Is like a cup athirst for wine of love;
Who sees and feels this meaning utterly,
The wrong of law, the right of man, the natural truth,
Partaking not of selfish aims, withholding not
The word that strengthens and the hand that helps!
Who wants and sympathizes with the pettiest life,
    And loves all things,
    And reaches up to God
    With thanks and blessing—
    He alone is living.
        —John Boyle O'Reilly

The sun gives forth to us heat and light rays, without which this old world could never be. Glory to warmth and light, which are power and wisdom shed upon us.

But there is likewise a third kind of ray shed by old Sol, whose mission we may not so readily bless. The sun's actinic rays are death-dealing. They cause disintegration, decomposition.

There are people who declare that time was when a great canopy of vapor hung over the earth and revolved with it, as Jupiter's vapory canopies now do; and that this vapory canopy kept off almost completely the actinic rays, while it admitted light and heat rays. Thus they account for Adam's and Methuselah's great ages. And they say that, unless this vapory canopy is again formed around our earth, to ward off these death-dealing rays, we shall never attain immortality in the flesh. They claim that as heat and light rays are power and wisdom, so the actinic rays are the Devil of the Bible, the Destroyer. And they believe that before man can be saved the Destroyer must be cast into outer darkness—shut out by that sheltering canopy of vapor.

An interesting and apparently plausible theory, is it not? But there are facts yet to be reckoned with. It is true that if a great watery veil spread itself over the earth to-day there might be no more death.

But neither could there be growth. Every form of life would continue as it is, wrinkles, gray hair and all. Why? Because there must be dissolution of old forms before there can be new ones made with that material. Take a photo plate as an instance: Here is a glass surface covered with a delicate gelatine; expose it in a dark-room under a red light and you can see just what it looks like; hold it there as long as you please and it still looks the same.

Now shut it into the black camera and sally forth on pleasure bent. The delicate film is undisturbed. But you come to a beautiful bit of woodland you want to "snap." You turn your focus upon it, and one little snap of a second's duration transforms that gelatine surface. Just for one instant of time you let in those actinic rays, and then all was darkness again inside the camera.

Now back you go into the dark-room and turn up the red light, by which you see again your beautiful bit of woodland, reproduced on that delicate gelatine surface. If you let in a bit of daylight your picture would be gone in a wink—the delicate gelatine would be "pied" in an attempt to reproduce whatever it faced. But you don't let in the light of day; you "fix" your bit of beautiful woodland by dipping the plate in a solution which hardens the particles of gelatine to the glass.

Henceforth the light cannot affect that gelatine; the picture you have, but life, progress, change, possibilities, are gone from the delicate gelatine forever.

But if you could live forever under a red light you would not need to "fix" your negative; it would forever retain that picture. And if you continued to live under the red light you might as well throw away your camera and plates—you could never take another picture. And you wouldn't need such amusement either—not for long. A few days in the red light and you would be sick, and a few more days and you would go mad. Finally nature would "fix" you, and there would be no more change. (I wonder if scientists have ever tried keeping a dead form hermetically sealed under red glass. The cutting off of the actinic rays ought to arrest decay and facial change.)

You see, the actinic rays, the devil or destroying rays of the sun, are absolutely essential to all change in the photo plate. Probably the actinic rays soften and separate the atoms of the gelatine, which are immediately polarized into the form of the scene it faces in the light and heat rays. Without the softening action of the actinic rays the gelatine could not take the form of the scene it faces; and without the light and heat rays it could not "see" and "feel" the scene, even if the actinic rays were present. It takes the trinity of rays, light, heat and actinic, to produce a photograph negative.

It is said that all inventions are but clumsy copies of mechanisms found in the human body and brain; that man contains on a microscopic scale all the inventions ever thought of, or that ever will be thought of. This is another way of saying that man is the microcosm, the universe the macrocosm. Victor Hugo expresses the same truth when he says "man is an infinite little copy of God."

The entire photographing process goes on in body and brain. Not a thought or sight but is photographed upon some tiny cell. Not a cell but may be cleaned of that impression, resensitized and given another impression.

Perhaps cells are immortal, as science claims. If so every cell must have undergone this cleaning, resensitizing and re-photographing process countless billions of times—with countless possibilities ahead.

And in every one of these picturings and repicturings the actinic rays are utterly indispensable. So, I cannot believe that the immortality of anything but a marble statue is dependent upon the cutting off of the sun's actinic rays. To be sure the actinic rays cause dissolution; but dissolution merely precedes resolution; dissolution gives light and heat (wisdom and love-power) a chance to produce yet higher forms.

Blessed be the destroying rays—blessed be nature's Devil; for he but clears the way for God himself, and cleans up and rearranges the rubbish after God has passed.

But when the race was in its childhood it looked upon the work done by these actinic rays, and fear was born. It saw things die; it saw destruction in the path of the wind; and like any child it imagined evil things. It personified the destroying power as Diablos, the Devil—which means destroyer.

It saw also the building, growing principle in nature and imagined a Builder.

But being a child it drew the childish conclusion that Destroyer and Builder worked eternally against each other, that they were enemies.

You see that was before the race had conceived the idea that two could work together; it was every man-savage for himself and the devil take the hindmost.

So the baby race began to love the Builder, God, and dislike and fear the Destroyer; and in its ignorance it personified both.

But here and there a clear-seer arose who glimpsed the truth. God spoke through Isaiah saying, "Behold, I make peace and I create evil; I, the Lord, do all these things." Solomon said the Lord "creates evil for the day of evil." And every seer of every Bible has tried to make clear the oneness, the all-wisdom all-power, all-presence of God.

All life is one. The sun is God manifest. The Destroyer belongs to the trinity and can no more be dispensed with than can the other two members, wisdom and love-power. And you may rest assured the Destroyer touches only that which needs dissolution that it may be transmuted.

Has anything gone out of your life? Have you lost that which you esteemed dear? Grieve not. It has been destroyed or taken away to make place for yet higher things.

God gives and God takes away in answer to your own highest desires. The Destroyer is but cleaning the plate for a more beautiful picture.

Be still and know that all things are working for the manifestation of your deepest desires. Work with things, not against them.

Chapter II: Three-Fold Being

Man is a three-strata being, instead of a two-strata one as Thomson J. Hudson theorizes. The obvious stratum is commonly called conscious or objective mind. This is the surface mind, the everyday mind, the mind we use in our waking hours.

Then there is the sub-conscious mind. The sub-conscious or subjective mind is the stratum of mind which receives the knowledge and wisdom which has passed through the conscious mind. The sub-conscious stratum of mind holds the habits and instincts formed at some time and place in and by the conscious mind. "Sub" means under; the sub-conscious mind lies under the conscious mind, as the depths of the lake lie under the surface.

But there is a third layer of mind which lies within and beyond both conscious and sub-conscious mind, and whose workings Hudson confounds with those of the sub-conscious mind. This may be called, for the lack of a better name, the super-conscious mind—the mind above conscious mind—the mind above consciousness.

This super-conscious mind is what we call God, out of which comes all wisdom.

Conscious mind is the point of contact between what we have already learned in this and previous states of existence, and the limitless reservoir of truth yet to be learned. Conscious mind is like unto the surface of a lake; sub-conscious mind is like the depths of the lake, every drop of which has at some time been on the surface, and is liable at any time to be recalled there; but super-conscious mind is like the rains of heaven and the streams from snow clad heights, whence the lake is perpetually replenished.

That which we already know, which we do by instinct, rests in the sub-conscious mind, ever ready to be recalled to the conscious mind. The conscious mind has to do with that which we are now learning. Super-conscious mind contains all wisdom, knowledge and power. In it we live and move and have our being and from it we are able to call, by aspiration and inspiration whatsoever we would know.

The visible universe as it is, is the sub-conscious and conscious mind of God; it represents what has been thought out of the universal reservoir of truth. But it is only a taste of the wonderful supplies still awaiting our aspiration and inspiration.

Think of all the wonderful discoveries and inventions of the last sixty years—all thought out of that great universal reservoir; and eye hath not seen nor ear heard the glories that yet await us in the great superconscious realm.

Mrs. Boehme illustrates individuality and solidarity by a star-shaped diagram. Each point of the star represents a person, a formed character; in other words, it represents the sub-conscious or habit self, the "nature" of the person. The center of the star represents God, the universal mind, with which every person is one on the unseen side. Looking at the points alone there is diversity, separateness; but looking from the center outward toward the points we see that points and center are all one, with no separating lines.

Now imagine a line cutting each point off from the center—an imaginary line, not a real one—and you will have a fair illustration of the conscious mind. The conscious mind lies between the personality and the universality of each of us; between the human and the divine of each; between what has been realized, and that limitless reservoir of beauties waiting to be realized.

Look at the star from the center and you will see that each point is simply a little bay projecting outward from the center; so each individuality is an inlet of God, each individual mind an inlet of divine mind.

And conscious mind is the imaginary line where personal mind and divine mind meet. You can readily see that one's conscious mind, then, would be filled with personality or divinity according as he looks down and is occupied with the "physical" being, or looks up and aspires toward the universal part of himself, the God part.

Now imagine the center of the star as being fluid, ever living and always free; and think of the points as being nearly solid, partially fixed. Imagine the points as containing water of life so muddy with false beliefs that it continually deposits along its edges layers of mud, ever hardening; with the water growing thicker and the beaches ever widening. Thus will you perceive the difference between personality and universality.

Now imagine the conscious mind endowed with will; note that when it turns toward the point of the star, toward the "material" part of itself, it becomes tense with anxiety and thus shuts off the point from the center, preventing a free play of the currents of life through the star-point, the personality. So the personality dries up, literally. This is the process by which we grow old.

Then imagine the conscious mind turned in faith and love toward the center of life—think, with this broader vision and knowledge of life, how lightly it would hold the things of personality, of that little point of personality; knowing that the personality is only a little inlet of divinity, and that the broad opening between the two is always open, that personality exists as a result of ever-flowing currents of divinity, and. that only his own grasping and straining can hinder the currents;—knowing all this, conscious mind turns away from the already realized personality and throws wide the opening into the great center of all life.

Thus conscious mind looks up, not down; and comes into his kingdom of love, wisdom, power. This is inspiration and aspiration. Yes, you may receive what you will, provided you call upon the super-conscious mind, the One mind over all. Whatsoever you can ask this mind believing you receive, you shall have.

When you can't ask in faith it is usually because you have not dwelt enough with the thought of God, the divine self of all creation. When we dwell much in the thought of personality, things, "materiality," then God seems faint and far away and impotent, and we can't believe we shall receive what we ask.

We need daily periods for withdrawing from the physical life and dwelling upon the thought of our oneness with omniscience, omnipotence, omnipresence, and our oneness with each other. Thus does faith grow, aspiration and inspiration become our mental habit, and the waters of life flow freely through us.

The One Spirit will guide you in all the affairs of life, and you are "safe" only when following its promptings.

If you would know the spirit's leadings, measure your impulses by the Golden Rule; for the spirit is Love to All.

Chapter III: Soul, Mind, and Body

If there is an individual soul that leaves the body at death, as most of us suppose, then this individual soul must be an organization of cell souls, just as the body is an organization of cells.

The body is referred to as the "shell," the "husk," the "house we live in," the "temple." In leaving the body, then, only the coarser elements are sloughed off and left as "dead," while the soul of every cell ascends, still organized in the individual soul; and the body cells disintegrate because the soul no longer holds them together.

This agrees with the statement of Theosophy that there is an "astral body" within the material body, which is like the material body but more beautiful. Many persons claim to have seen this astral body leave its "temple." Perhaps Paul meant this when he spoke of two bodies.

It seems reasonable to suppose that this spiritual body carries within it all knowledge gained in this state of being, and that in a new generation the older experiences are "forgotten," just as a thousand things are forgotten every day of our lives—things which at some future time we may recall. The thing was there, in our sub-consciousness, all the time; it simply did not affect us strongly enough to make us think about it.

A child's interest in this generation keeps in the background of sub-consciousness its memories of past generations. If it wanted to hard enough, and thought about it enough, it could recall incidents in previous generations just as it can recall an incident of yesterday or last year which it has temporarily forgotten.

Many people claim to have recalled past states of existence by desire and concentration, and many claim to have flashes of remembrance without any special desire or intention. And the Society for Psychical Research has on record many strange cases of dual or many-sided personality, etc., which seem to confirm this conception of soul and body.

It seems to me that the soul is the naked life force which is one with spirit; that material experiences are the matrices by which the life force, or soul force, is formed and organized into individuality; and that we shed the "material" parts of the body as fast as we can—just as in the lower forms of life shells are discarded when backbones appear; the shell protecting and moulding the life-form until it is sufficiently formed and organized to do without the shell.

When the physical body becomes too stiff and un- yielding a form for the growing mind or soul, then it is discarded. And it looks as if the soul, through growth and attraction, steps into a new generation where the material at hand will afford it a better matrix.

As long as the body is alive and yielding, responding readily to the developing organization of the individual, the soul keeps changing in its matrix, its body, day by day as needed; but a stiff, too-rigid and old-style matrix or body has to be discarded in whole, for a new one. "From the soul the bodye forme doth take," and when the body becomes inadequate to express the soul growth it is sloughed off altogether.

The body, astral and material, is the storage of the past experiences and the wisdom organized through those experiences.

The "objective mind," in the brain, is the surface of this storage, the doorway by which all this wisdom and knowledge entered into individual organization. The brain is the switchboard by which we are able to use this store of wisdom and knowledge at will.

The "objective mind" governs and directs not only the switchboard, but all the sub-stores with which it connects.

The "objective mind" also connects with the universal storehouse of wisdom, upon which it draws by what we call "intuition." It is through this connection with the universal that we are enabled to "rise higher than our source" of sub-conscious wisdom and knowledge gained in previous generations. In order to grow we need the super-conscious wisdom which is All.

Just as by desire and concentration we can recall the knowledge and wisdom gained in previous generations, so by desire and concentration directed toward the Universal, the Infinite, we call to us yet greater wisdom and knowledge than any yet realized.

The body which disintegrates after death is a mere collection of cell-cocoons from which the organized cell- souls have flown to new states of being. With its soul the body loses its feeling, the atoms disintegrating, each becoming what it was before, simply a bit of "dead matter" which is not dead at all.

The atoms of matter are just the same after death as before; but the organizing and in-forming spirit and soul, spirit or soul (for there is no dividing line between them), has departed, leaving each atom to live its little life again without relation to other atoms Without this organizing spirit to draw and hold the atoms together they fall apart—"ashes to ashes."

The cell is the unit organization of the body, each cell clothed with many atoms. The soul of the cell leaves it, just as the soul leaves the body as a whole.

That the astral body is an organization of cell souls, just as the physical body is an organization of cells, I have no present doubt.

And it looks reasonable to me to suppose that the soul, or astral body, carries within it all the records of all the individual's experiences since the beginning of time. That with every generation and experience this astral grows in wisdom and knowledge and beauty of character, I see no reason to doubt.

And by the power of universal attraction it is drawn in each new generation, to the exact parentage and condition it needs to help its growth in grace.

Chapter IV: How to Aim

To Life, the force behind the Man, intellect is a necessity, because without it he blunders into death. Just as Life, after ages of struggle, evolved that wonderful bodily organ, the eye, so that the living organism could see where it was going and what was coming to help or threaten it, and thus avoid a thousand dangers that formerly slew it, so it is evolving today a mind's eye that shall see, not the physical world, but the purpose of Life, and thereby enable the individual to work for that purpose instead of thwarting and baffling it by setting up shortsighted personal aims as at present.

Even as it is, only one sort of man has ever been happy, has ever been universally respected among all the conflicts of interests and illusions …

I sing, not arms and the hero, but the philosophic man; he who seeks in contemplation to discover the inner will of the world, in invention to discover the means of fulfilling that will, and in action to do that will by the so-discovered means.

—Bernard Shaw.

Without definiteness of aim nothing can be accomplished.

With too definite an aim very little can be accomplished.

This is the paradox of all accomplishment. It looks hard, but is in reality very easy—so easy that a child lives it.

The key to the problem is this: No man liveth unto himself and none dieth unto himself; we are all members one of another; all creation moves to "one far-off divine event," the definite details of which no human being has yet grasped. Perhaps none ever will grasp it. For how can the hand or the foot conceive the structure and purposes of the whole body?

There is a Universal Aim which includes and impels all individual aims. There is one great intelligence, one spirit, one purpose actuating every human being. The "Plan of Salvation" is not a mere superstitious myth. There certainly is a "plan," a "divine event," which we are all working at, whether we know it or not.

There is a Divine Ideal beckoning us every one. Glimpses of it are caught even by the fool who hath said in his heart there is no God, no oneness of life and purpose.

As our bodies are all members of God's body, so our ideals are members of the Universal Ideal; our aims are members of the Universal Aim.

Your hand may understand and define its impulse to grasp or release; but can it understand and define your aim and purpose, which gave it the impulse?

We can imagine the hand understanding its own movements, but can it understand your movements and purposes? The hand says, "I want to grasp this"; but can it in any sense understand your purpose, which made it want to grasp?

So you say, "I want to paint pictures." or "I want to make money," or "I want to teach school," or "I want to be a home-keeper and mother," or "I want to build bridges." But can you tell why you want to do these things or others?

Can you define the Great I *want* of which your I want is but an outcropping? Can you see the Universal Ideal of which your ideal is a detail? No; you can see your individual I want, but the Universal I *want* is too large for you to take in from your point of view.

Did you ever say to yourself, "I want to be a bridge builder"; then after you had become a successful bridge builder did you find yourself rather disgusted with the bridge business? Did you find yourself saying, "I want to be a painter instead of a bridge builder"? And you couldn't imagine why your wants wouldn't stay satisfied with bridge building.

Can you imagine the hand being disgusted because after it had grasped the book awhile it found itself wanting to let go? Of course. The hand would not understand why it could not remain "constant" to its first desire: it would not see the reason for letting go.

So with us members of the "Stupendous Whole."

Universal purpose and desire play through us. We know we "want" this and we "don't want" that. When we are on the "animal" plane we simply gratify our wants when we can, and are satisfied until another want impels us. By and by we begin to reason about our wants. We call some of them "good," and gratify them if we can. We call some of them "bad" and fight them with all our puny might—and are correspondingly unhappy. In both cases we fail to see why we want what we want.

When after we have learned to build bridges we find ourselves wanting to paint pictures we resist the desire and keep on building bridges. Then, if the Universal Purpose really wants us to stop building bridges and make pictures it keeps on impelling us in the new direction until we finally find a way to get at the painting. If we are too stubborn the Universal I *want* gets us out of the way and raises up our sons and daughters to paint the pictures.

It is like this: In response to the Universal I *want* you have taught your good right hand to thread needles and sew, until it can almost do it in the dark. All the nerves and brains and muscles in your finger tips have learned that little trick. Now, in response to a new Universal I *want*, you decide that that good right hand of yours is to learn to run scales on the piano.

You sit down at the piano, place your hand in position and impel it to strike the notes. But this sort of thing is entirely new to your fingers! Every little muscle is stiff, every nerve and every tiny bit of finger-brain protests that it can't run scales!—it doesn't know how!—its work is sewing—it can't, so there! You say to yourself, "How stiff my fingers are, and how rebellious —they won't mind me at all!"

But you keep on sending your want, your will into them. You "practice" long hours every day. And by and by you find your fingers have learned the new trick and can do it without special thought and will from you. You kept pouring your want into that hand until it became the hand's want and will. From working against your want the hand has come to work with it and by it.

Why did you do it? Because the Universal I *want* kept pouring itself into you until you took up the practice; just as you poured the I *want* on into your hands until they, too, wanted to do it, and did it.

Were your fingers extra rebellious? Did they fight, and get tangled up, and imitate each other's movements? Then what did you do with them?

You kept them at it; and you kept them at it a great deal longer time than you would if they had been more obedient fingers; you kept them practicing until they learned to do the work willingly, with interest, artistically. Then you gave them beautiful things to play with, instead of hard things to work at.

Of course the beautiful things to play with are all made up of the very same sort of things your fingers have been working hard at. But the monotony of repetition is all gone from the beautiful play. It is joy to play. It is "hard work" to practice scales.

But without all those scales there can never be a satisfying play. In practice we learn by repetition to do well and gracefully one thing at a time. In play we string all these movements together in a satisfying play of joy and praise.

We hope for the perfection of action which alone makes satisfying play possible; therefore we keep practicing. The harder our fingers rebel, the longer and more persistently we keep them at it—that is all.

Now the Universal I *want* keeps us at things in precisely the same way. The Universal is working out a glorious Ideal of perfect play, wherein every member of itself shall be shining, obedient, supple enough to play with grace and full joy the "music of the spheres."

You and I being more or less stiff and disobedient and dense have to be kept at our practices until we learn to do them right. We say, "Oh, if I could only get into my right niche; but I seem to be held here in spite of all I can do!" We say we "don't like" the sort of "drudgery" we are "condemned" to—there must be something "wrong" with the universe, or with economic or family conditions, or we would not have to drudge at one kind of thing when we are "fitted" for something else, or want to do something else.

Our fingers cry out in the same way when we keep them at the scales—"Oh," they cry, "why are we compelled to this dreary commonplace repetition when our souls long for beautiful harmonies?"

You see, it never occurs to them that they are "compelled" to this commonplace scale practice because they long for beautiful harmonies and happy play.

And it doesn't occur readily to you and to me that we are held to our dish washing, our business routine, our bridge building because our souls long for greater things.

But it is so. The perfection of large ideals can never be attained except through perfection of detail; and through the dish washing, business routine, bridge building, we are perfecting the details of self-command, of body and brain control which will enable us to play the great harmonies our souls already feel.

The great things we feel and desire without being able to express them, comprise the Universal Ideal at which every soul is aiming, whether or not he knows it.

The perfection of this great Ideal we see as through smoked glass, darkly. We get all sorts of half-views of it, and spend a lot of time squabbling about it. But not one of us really knows even a tiny part of the glory and beauty and joy of that Universal Ideal, which includes and actuates all our personal ideals. "It doth not yet appear what we shall be." But we know that when the Great Ideal does appear we shall all have our places in the joy of its beauty, for every one of us will have had his place and done his part in working out that ideal.

The Universal Ideal is gently urging us on to ineffable good. But none of us can conceive the details of the good which is yet to appear. We are all hoping and working for this "Indeterminate Good," as Hanford Henderson calls it.

It constitutes our large Ideal, which includes all our lesser, fleeting ideals and even our passing wishes and longings.

It is with our large ideals that definiteness of aim is a mistake- An "indeterminate good" necessitates a general aim. It will not do to say "I know exactly where the blossoms will appear when the earth blossoms as a rose, and I know exactly the day they will appear; therefore will I till only those exact spots and get my ascension robes ready for that exact hour."

The man who is so dead sure of his great aim will sooner or later, like "Perkins" in "Quincy Adams Sawyer," find himself perched on the ridgepole with his white robes flapping in the cold night and his goods in somebody else's possession. When one is too sure of the "far-off divine event" he muddles the present opportunity for hastening that event.

"Wisdom is before him that hath understanding; but the eyes of a fool are in the ends of the earth." The man who is too sure of the "indeterminate good" misses the present good. The man who aims at the Great Good which he cannot hit, misses the little Goods, near at hand, which need to be hit.

What should we think of a hunter who aimed only at big game beyond his gun's reach, while small game gamboled at his feet? We'd think him a fool who deserved to starve to death. Of course.

We miss our chances by straining after the big game beyond our reach.

The great ideal should have our faith, rather than our aim.

Aim only at that which is within reach, and trust the big things to time and the spirit.

You stand in the Now. Keep your aim for the things of the Now. Thus will your aim gain accuracy and you will be ready for the Great Things when they shall at last appear in the Now.

Where are you Now? Are you building bridges? Then aim to build this one better than any other was ever built. Aim to improve your work now.

Aim to enjoy it all; for only as joy brightens you can you see how to better your work and methods.

And proficiency at bridge building means freedom to follow your next ideal. The greater your proficiency the nearer the top you get, and the more money you get for your work; and the more money you have the more time you can take for working out your next ideal.

In proportion as you are progressively proficient at your work your money stream will increase. In proportion as you enjoy your work you will grow in efficiency and money. The drudge is held to his work because he does not put into it the love and interest and joy necessary to make him progressively proficient.

He says "lack of money keeps him from getting into a new line of work." That is it exactly—the Universal Spirit which urges us on keeps the money away from us until we have gained in this thing the proficiency needed to fit us for other work.

Are you building bridges and at the same time aiming to paint pictures? And are you too poor to drop the bridge building and devote all your time to painting pictures?

Then I say unto you have faith in your desire to paint pictures, for your desire is an outcropping of Universal Desire and is certain to find its satisfaction. Your desire is the desire of Omnipotence, Omniscience, which will in no wise disappoint itself. All desires shall be fulfilled in the fullness of time.

Would you hasten the time? Then have faith in your desire; but aim at the bridge building. Do better and better the work you find to do until the way opens to a new line of work.

And do every detail of your bridge building as if it were the painting of the greatest picture. Think you that accuracy of observation, delicacy of touch, harmony of thought and power of expression are gained only by dabbling paint on a canvas with a camel's-hair brush? No. Bridge building has its place in training a great painter. Put your soul into it while you are held to it, and give it its full chance to do the work.

Have faith in your desire to paint pictures, but aim your energies at the bridge you are building now. Keep your faith high, your aim true, and verily in an hour when you least expect it the way will open from bridge building to picture painting.

Chapter V: The Substance of Things

Where are the cowards who bow down to environment—
Who think they are made of what they eat, and must conform to the bed that they lie in?
I am not wax,—I am energy!
Like the whirlwind and waterspout, I twist my environment into my form, whether it will or not.
What is it that transmutes electricity into auroras, and sunlight into rainbows, and soft flakes of snow into stars, and adamant into crystals, and makes solar systems of nebulae?
Whatever it is, I am its cousin-german.
I, too, have my ideas to work out, and the universe is given me for raw material.
I am a signet, and I will put my stamp upon the molten stuff before it hardens.
What allegiance do I owe to environment? I shed environments for others as a snake sheds its skin.
The world must come my way,—slowly, if it will,—but still my way.
I am a vortex launched in chaos to suck it into shape.
  —Ernest Crosby.

"To a certain extent I have been benefited by these teachings. In some ways they do not appear to have a very practical result. It is possible to concentrate and obtain small things, but any real change of surroundings seems to be quite dependent upon circumstances entirely outside my own will." H. B.

Thus writes a shortsighted and faithless one—faithless because of her shortsightedness. Another woman who has observed the same things writes thus: "If I see no great results now I know it is because I am working for large things."

Life "concentrates" on a mushroom and grows it in a night; but an oak requires twenty years of "concentration." A woman "concentrates" on a good dinner, a bit of sewing, the control of her tongue for an hour, $5.00 for a new hat, the cure of a headache, and success crowns each effort. These are little things, the mushrooms of an hour, used shortly and soon forgotten.

The same woman "concentrates" for a complete change in disposition or environment, for anything in fact which seems a long way off from present conditions. Now, if she is a shortsighted woman she has little or no faith in anything which she cannot see, hear, taste, smell or feel. She can see, taste and smell a mushroom, so she believes in it. She could see an oak and believe in that. But she cannot see the acorn growing underground; therefore she has no faith that there is an oak growing. And if there is already a little oak in sight she cannot see it grow, no matter how steadily she looks at it; therefore she "fears" the oak is not growing.

But the far-seeing woman is different. She sees through things. She feels the intangible. She hears, smells, and tastes that which moves upon the face of the deep and brings forth things. She touches the true substance (that which stands under) of things which are to be.

Her faith rests in invisible life; the other woman's faith rests only in the visible things which life has made.

To say that H. B. has no faith would be an untruth. Every living being is full of faith, or he could not live.

Faith is in the atmosphere and we live by using it, just as a fish lives by using the water. Faith springs eternal in every human breast, fed from the universal source. To talk of one's little faith or one's much faith is like talking of the earth's squareness.

Every soul lives by faith and plenty of it. But he lives by faith in what? There's the rub.

Until we emerge from a sense of materiality—and no one has as yet got more than his nose above these muddy waters— we live by faith in things seen, smelt, tasted, heard and felt. These are the only things we are familiar with; to them we pin our faith, and pride ourselves upon our good sense, reason and lack of "superstition."

"I can't believe in anything unless I can see it" is our self-satisfied cry; "you can't fool me with your religious hocus-pocus, nor with your rabbit's foot and horseshoe and four-leaved clover; I can see no connection between a rabbit's foot and your good luck, therefore I know no connection exists; I can see no big God on a great white throne, consequently I know none exists; show me your God; show me the string which connects the four-leaved clover to your good luck and I'll put my faith in it."

The material one reckons without his Unseen Host. By and by the Unseen begins to juggle with him. His beautiful plans, every step of which he could plainly see, are blown awry. He can't see why! The things in which he had such faith begin to totter and tumble about his ears. He can't see why! Reluctantly he begins to see that there are mighty forces he can't see. His whole beautiful material world begins to dance to strings he can't see!

Ah, so there are things he can't see, hear, smell, taste or feel! They may be a fearful and chaotic jumble; they seem to be; but they are there, after all his certainty that he could see, smell, hear, taste and feel The Whole Thing.

And he begins to reach out toward these unseen things. He peers and peers into the darkness and stillness. And as he peers his faiths gradually loosen their hold upon the old visible things and begin to reach out into the darkness and silence.

He sends his faiths groping, groping, feeling their way through the Invisible, always seeking the strings to which visible things have been dancing and tumbling.

At first all is darkness; but by and by faith gets its tentacles around Something Unseen;—ah, there is Something which disposes what man proposes—an unseen, un-tasted, unheard, un-smelt, unfelt Something.

A terrible Something it may be, but still a Something, all-powerful, all-present. He has sent his feelers into the Invisible and touched God, the soul, the life-principle, which makes and unmakes, gives and takes away all those little things to which he was wont to pin his faiths.

The next thing is to find out the nature of this mighty Something whose home is in the Invisible. But how find out the nature of the Unseen? Not by touch, taste, smell, sight or hearing—not at first anyway. But by its fruits you may know a tree to be good or bad.

By its fruits you may know the invisible powers to be beneficent or malefic. And the material one is familiar with fruits, with things. He built such beautiful things himself, so he ought to be a judge of the fruits of labor. The fruits of his labor were all good, he knows they were. If only the great Unseen had not spoiled them all! Oh, the labors of the Unseen brought his own good efforts to naught—the Unseen must be a terrible and evil power; its fruits are destruction of his own good buildings. He fears this Great Unseen Power to which his faiths are beginning to pin themselves.

But wait: Good is beginning to rise from the ashes of his ruins. This so terrible calamity is turning out a blessing! New and greater things are forming, to take the places of the lost fruits! And they are good.

Oh, this Great Unseen works in terrifying mystery but its fruits are good.

Now he is ready to "come unto God." He begins to see the un-seeable things, and his faiths tendril them.

Those who would "come unto Him must believe that He is, and that He is a rewarder of them that diligently seek Him."

Those who would understand and feel and use the invisible forces must believe that they are, and that they reward those who diligently seek to understand and use them.

The Unseen things move the visible world. The material one being pinned by his faiths to the things of the world is moved as the world is moved. He is a mere puppet in the hands of the Unseen powers.

As he looses the faiths which bound him to the world rack, and sends his faith tendrils into the Unseen, he becomes one with the powers which pull the world-strings.

"Faith is the sub-stance (the underlying and creating principle) of things hoped for, the evidence of things not seen."

The material one's faith is pinned to things already seen; therefore, his creative principle is poured into the thing already created.

Then Life juggles and tumbles things until the material one's faiths are torn loose from their material moorings, and go feeling out into the Unseen for new things to cling to. When the whole bunch of visible things has failed us; when houses, lands, money, friends, and even fathers and mothers and brothers and sisters have gone back on us, what is there left to pin our faiths to? And without something to have faith in how could we live at all?

We couldn't live without faiths to steady us; witness the suicides and the deaths from broken hearts.

And if all visible things have failed us, if our faiths are broken loose from fathers, mothers, brothers, friends, houses and lands, where else can our faiths take hold again except in the region of the Unseen?—the region where "the wind bloweth whither it listeth and thou canst hear the sound thereof but canst not tell whence it cometh nor whither it goeth;" the region of substance, of creative power.

It seems very terrible to have our faiths broken loose from fathers, mothers, brothers, friends, houses and lands; but it is good for us, as time always proves.

Broken loose from the effects of creative energy, our faiths reach out into the Unseen and tendril the very energy itself. From a state of oneness with things we evolve a new being at one with the creative power within things.

What are the unseen things to which our torn faiths begin to attach themselves? Our faith itself is unseen, the sub-stance of things hoped for, the substantial evidence of things not yet seen.

What do we hope for that we have not yet seen?

First of all we hope for peace—another of the substantial unseen things. We hope for love, the most substantial of unseen things. Oh, if we had but peace and love we could count all else well lost! And behold, by unseen faith tendrils our bruised faiths attach themselves to the unseen substance of peace and love.

Wisdom is an unseen substance—our unseen faiths attach themselves to the unseen source of wisdom. Thought is unseen; our faiths, torn loose from things, begin to reach out into the unseen realm of thought. Ideals are unseen things. Our faiths, torn loose from the already-realized, begin to tendril the unseen ideals, the race's ideals, the family ideals, and lastly our individual ideals.

Our unseen faiths become one with these unseen ideals; and through these little faith tendrils we begin literally to draw the ideal down into our physical being and out into the visible world.

Through our faith tendrils the ideal is literally ex-pressed, pressed out into visibility.

When our faiths were attached to material things, the material things (being negative to us) sucked us dry. Now our faith tendrils reach upward to the unseen ideal realm of real substance (to which we are negative) and by the same law of dynamics it is we who draw the life; draw it from the unseen realm of real life substance.

Of ourselves we could do nothing—the things to which our faiths attached us sucked us dry of power, and the unseen powers finally tore us loose; but now that we are tendriled by our faiths to the Unseen, "the Father" in us and through us doeth the works of rightness that bring peace.

And behold, we are filled with the unseen power, and through our faith in the Unseen we pass on the fruits of the spirit, which are "love, joy, peace, longsuffering, gentleness, meekness, faith, temperance."

And being filled with the power of the Unseen we pass on the fruits of the spirit to fathers, mothers, brothers, friends, houses, lands; pass it on in every act of life and in every breath we take.

We breathe out that which, through our faith-tendrils, the Great Unseen breathes into us.

Then, behold, that which is written comes to pass: "Ye shall have an hundredfold more houses and lands and fathers and mothers and brothers in this present time." You shall have them to use at will.

While you were attached by your faiths to things they used you; now you use them.

Pin your faiths to the Unseen things and let patience have her perfect work. So shall you realize your heart's full desire. Let things rock as they will; let facts be stubborn and conditions hard if need be. Never mind them. To mind them is to pin your faiths to them.

Mind the Unseen things. Pin your faiths to your ideals.

Flout facts and hard conditions! Believe in the Unseen.

Train your faiths upward.

"Whatsoever ye desire believe that ye receive," and you shall surely have it.

If it is a mushroom expect it in a night. If you desire a great oak give it time to grow. In due time, perhaps in an hour when you least expect it, it will surely appear.

The one thing needful is to pin your little faiths to the Unseen Source of all things.

Believe in the great unseen part of yourself and the universal.

Chapter VI: To Get at the Substance

All desirable and as-yet-unexpressed things are in the silence waiting to be drawn into expression through aspiration and inspiration.

Of course one can aspire and inspire anywhere and under almost any conditions. I remember one great aspiration of mine which was satisfied whilst I was sitting in a crowded street car with folks standing in front of me and others clinging to the running board.

The Things of the Silence are everywhere present, permeating solid things as the X-rays do. All creation cannot hinder a man communing with the Unseen at any time and in any place—all creation cannot hinder him except as he lets it.

But that is the trouble—he lets it interfere unless he is in almost agonizing earnest about the unseen things. That momentous hour on the crowded street car came after weeks of most earnest "seeking,'" after weeks of almost constant "concentrating" on this one thing I wanted to receive from the Unseen. I was so absorbed in that one subject that the crowds were as nothing to me.

In order to get anything—wisdom, power, love—from the silence one's whole interest must be absorbed in the matter.

Your interest is like the plate in a camera; it receives impressions only from that upon which it is turned. And the camera must be held steadily in one position until the impression is received.

The human camera receives impressions from the unseen in exactly the same way that it receives impressions from the seen world.

But it takes a longer time to receive a complete impression from the unseen, just as it takes a longer time to get a good negative in the dark.

The unseen is the dark to us; hence the long time it often takes to get a complete impression of anything we desire to receive in the silence. It takes a longer "exposure" to get the impression.

"Concentration" is merely the steady "exposure" of the attention, the interest, to the thing we desire to realize, to make tangible.

Now the busy person, the person who is interested in a thousand things, keeps his interest so busy taking instantaneous photographs that he has no time to get impressions from the unseen. His mind is constantly flitting from one thing to another. When it happens to turn toward the unseen it simply sweeps the dark quickly and comes back to earth again without an impression.

Instead of a steady aspiration toward the ideal there is a constant perspiration toward the real.

As there is nothing new under the sun the only progress made is around and around the same old things.

The only real relief from things as they are lies in the unseen.

The only way to get at the relief is to "concentrate" on the unseen things. In order to do this the attention must be called away from seen things. The mind must be "set on things above," and kept set until the "renewing" is complete.

People who are not yet satisfied that the visible world does not and cannot satisfy, will see no need of going into the silence on set occasions. And there is another class who are apt to see no need of it—the class whose "concentration" on the invisible is so constant that material things assume the subordinate relation. These are people who have "got the truth" by coming up through great tribulation; who have run the gamut of things and found the principle behind things.

And almost invariably, if not always (I have never heard of an exception), these are people who have tried nearly every method of spiritual culture extant, have practiced fasting and prayer, breath exercises, denials and affirmations, and treatments and concentrations of every conceivable kind.

Martin Luther was one of these; and at last, when he had tried everything else and was crawling up the church steps on all fours, he "found the truth." Immediately he arose, repudiated all his good works as unavailing, and went about praising and preaching that not by works but by faith we are healed.

Eight or ten years ago I heard Paul Militz, who had worked for years at all manner of spiritual, mental and breath exercising, repudiate it all as "unnecessary." "Not any of these things avails you," he said. And others who have "found the truth" reiterate the same statement.

And yet every one of them has "found the truth" through those very practices.

If Martin Luther had stopped short of crawling up those church steps as his own seeking spirit bade him, he would never have "found the truth." If Militz, Shelton, Burnell, et al., had left out one of their practices they would still be "seeking."

The spirit in every man bids him do things and refrain from doing other things, in order to "save" him self from something or other. Is this universal urge only a lie? No.

These concentration exercises are kindergarten methods by which we learn to use ourselves. When by practice we have learned how, we discard the kindergarten methods. What was gained by self-conscious effort becomes habit. We turn intuitively to the unseen, whereas we used to turn to it only by conscious effort, by special practices.

But why repudiate the practices? Why tell others who are trying to learn how, that their efforts are all useless? By practices we found the way; why discourage practice?

There are people who as yet are wrapped up in the material. There are those who are wrapped up in the unseen. Neither of these are in present need of set times for "concentrating" upon the unseen, the ideal side of life.

But there is a third great "middle class" who are not absorbed in the already manifest world, and who want to be one with the unseen world of causation. To these I say, follow the example of all the "adepts" of all the ages; practice "concentration."

To all who want to accomplish something I say, Go into the silence regularly for power and wisdom to accomplish.

To those whose interests are mainly in the material world, but who want to understand and be deeply interested in the unseen world—from whence come all things,—to those I say, Go into the silence at regular periods every day.

To all humanity who are longing for Something, I say. All things are in the Silence; be still and know.

Chapter VII: The Spirit and the Individual

"I was washing my breakfast dishes one morning when it occurred to me to go to visit a friend who lived several miles away. I did my work and started to dress for my journey, when there came over me such a feeling of depression, or despondency, or gloom, that I could not understand. I kept on getting ready, all the time trying to reason away the feeling. But it would not go. Finally I got my hat on and one glove and started for the door, when such a heaviness came over me that I turned back into my room and sat down saying, 'God, I want to know what the meaning is of all this.'

The answer came loud, strong and firm, 'Stay at home.' I stayed, and taking off my hat, gloves and cape I felt so light I seemed to walk on air. At the time I supposed the voice (I call it voice for want of a more definite term) had told me to stay at home because some one was coming to me for help. This was my first year as a teacher and healer. But not a soul came that day, nor that night, and the thought flitted through my mind that perhaps it was all nonsense after all and I might as well have gone.

Well, the outcome was that the train I would have taken met with a fearful accident in which many were killed or badly injured. This is only one of many similar experiences I have had. I do not stop to reason out things. The world has tried for 1900 years to follow reason, and look at the outcome I follow my intuition and it never fails me."

—Flora P. Howard, Los Angeles, Cal.

One's reason is not a thing to be belittled and denied. It is his crowning glory, created for use.

But it is not all the wisdom a man has access to, nor is it the greatest. The man who exalts his understanding above the wisdom of the rest of creation, and un-creation, is a fool and sure to come to grief.

But he who rejoices in his personal understanding or reason as the means by which he taps the source of all wisdom, is in a fair way to profit by his own intelligence and the universal intelligence besides.

Everybody knows his foresight is not so good as his hindsight. He has demonstrated the fact many a time, by as many little tumbles off his high horse. Really, it seems as if he might have learned by this time not to be quite so sure about his reason.

After Mrs. Howard knew that the train she meant to go on had been wrecked she saw, plainly, why it was unwise for her to go on that particular train. Her reason had been enlightened, her hindsight perfected.

By what? By universal intelligence.

Suppose New York City should set itself up as the center of all wisdom—suppose she were to say, "What I cannot reason out is not worth knowing." Suppose she continued to send out decrees into all the world, but turned up her nose at the messages sent in to her. What do you suppose would happen? She would go to smash in a week. It is by her reception of all those messages as to outside doings, that she is enabled to reason out her business problems and send out messages that move the world. To exalt New York knowledge and reason, and despise outside knowledge and reason, would quickly ruin her.

Intuition is the wireless line by which we receive directions from every other station in the universe. After Mrs. Howard had received and obeyed her message from the universal—some days after—she knew why she had been so directed.

He who is puffed up in his own conceit is eternally despising his intuitions, following his back-number reasons, and getting into the "accidents." Then he wonders why he is so abused.

You see, we have none of us ever passed this way before. This day is a new day; this bit of road has never been traveled before. Nobody can know by reason what we shall run into just around the bend there. He may make a rough guess at it, but he cannot know.

But—there is Something which, whether it knows or does not know consciously, what is, or will be, around that corner there—there is Something which can and does send us by the wireless line a message to keep away, or to go to it, as the case may be.

Now Mrs. Howard was a woman with no desire to be in such a smash, and she believed her intuitions would keep her warned away from them.

Now next door to Mrs. Howard there may have lived another woman, just as "good" as Mrs. Howard, just as devoted to her intuitions, who received a message to go on that train. At the same moment Mrs. Howard's heart grew heavy and she heard the message, "Stay at home," this other woman's heart grew light and she heard the message, "Go." So she went blithely forth to the train. She mounted the steps and walked into the car and along past several vacant seats before she felt the impression to sit down. She sat down and gazed happily out of the window.

By and by, as they were bowling swiftly along there came a sudden crash, and shrieks, and hiss of steam. Then there was work to do.

This woman neighbor of Mrs. Howard's, beyond a little shaking up from which she almost instantly recovered, was entirely uninjured. There were dead and dying in front and behind her, but she was safe. There was work to do and she was there to do it.

You see, this woman was a physician and surgeon, and the only one on the train. She had been years preparing for such work, and she believed her intuitions would lead her, strong and well herself, into just such opportunities as this. So the message which depressed Mrs. Howard brought light to the soul of this woman.

Each received and interpreted the message according to her own particular character.

And what about the injured and killed? They too were "led by the spirit." Each by his own self-built character related himself to his particular "fate." I wouldn't wonder if a good many of them did it by filling up on the accident and criminal columns of the daily papers. The man who thinks in terms of accident is pretty sure to meet them.

But probably more of the "victims" were drawn through their false religion. The man who thinks himself (who really thinks it, "in his heart")—who thinks himself a "vile worm" and a great sinner deserving of a "bad end," and yet who has not "repented," is daily relating himself more closely to all sorts of violent and horrible things.

And everywhere and at all times the violent man, the strenuous man, no matter how "good" he may be, is preparing himself to be led into whatever catastrophe fits him.

There is no hit and miss about our "fates"—we get just what we are fitted for.

And through all ages we have been fitting ourselves; and we are still at it. He who is not busy fitting himself for the best is relating himself to the less good.

He who fits himself to die with his boots on will die so. He who fits himself for "accidents" will die by an accident. He who fits himself for life may perchance never again see death.

When the bubonic plague is about to appear in a place all the birds fly away. What warned them? Oh, that was only "instinct"—something common, that we wise beings never use.

Before Mt. Pelee spit destruction, all the wild animals (not one of which could have had any personal knowledge, or any record of volcano lore) fled from the vicinity. The tame animals whimpered and cowered and those which could ran away. Then the people's hearts began to sink and the most ignorant of them ran after the animals. As Mt. Pelee grew more emphatic in her prophecies all hearts grew heavier and heavier and all souls heard the message "Go."

Then there was hurried preparation for a hasty exodus. But no; the wise, educated, sensible men put their heads together and decided that they would not and others should not be guided by any such common thing as "instinct," or by their own sinking hearts. No! Even though their hearts fell into their shoes and their knees knocked and their teeth chattered they would be sensible, they would; they'd use their divine reason, they would—Mt. Pelee had never destroyed them before and it wouldn't now.

So the wise reasoners corralled the poor fools. And they were well corralled. Only one ever got away.

Now just what this spirit is like that tries to lead us into all truth, is a thing I don't know. But that there is such a spirit that pervades and would save all creatures from harm I do know, both by intuition (the spirit's witness with my spirit) and by actual and repeated experiences of both kinds. I have been led of the spirit into ways of pleasantness, peace and plenty; and before that I turned up my nose at the spirit and went my own way into all sorts of troubles.

And I have a theory, based on the spirit's witness with mine, as to what this spirit is and how it acts.

The spirit is the universal intelligence which fills this universe so full there is not room for anything else. There are just little eddies and whirls and currents and cross-currents in this great ocean of intelligence. And you are one eddy in it, and I another; and each of us sets up little swirls and currents that move us about and move other things to us. And when a leaf floats by it is drawn into our eddy, but when we swirl by a rock, the rock in unmoved and so are we. We are not related to the rock.

When gold is placed beside a horseshoe magnet it stays put. The magnet and gold are not interested in each other. But that does not prove that the magnet is stupid and dead. No, there is a great current of longing in that magnet. If it had means of locomotion it would go about the world seeking, seeking—perhaps never knowing just what it was seeking, but still seeking. And by and by it would begin to feel a definite inclination to go in a certain direction.

Now if it is just a fool magnet without great pride in its brains it will follow that definite inclination. And as it journeys the drawing power will grow, and it will journey faster, and behold, it will fly into the arms of its affinity, a steel bar. And it will cling and cling, and the bar will cling, and joy will be born.

It takes two, and an exchange of intelligence, to bring joy into being.

Or perhaps our magnet will stay at home and long, long, until it draws to it steel filings.

This is not so fanciful as you may suppose. All things are intelligent. All things are putting their little compulsions on all creation for satisfaction. And in due time all compulsions will be met. The great sea is seething with intelligence, and affinities are coming together.

It is the attraction of the magnet for the steel that constitutes what I call the spirit. That attraction is intelligence.

When in doubt as to the meaning of your solar center feelings, do nothing. Come back as Mrs. Howard did, sit down; be still; ask for the meaning; and obey.

Chapter VIII: By Crooked Paths

The Rev. R. F. Horton tells a little story of a remarkable answer to prayer.
He was with a party of tourists in Norway. In exploring some wild and marshy country one of the ladies lost one of her "goloshes." The overshoe could not be replaced short of Bergen, at the end of their tour, and it was out of the question to attempt to explore that wild country without rubbers. The golosh must be found, or the tour curtailed.

As you may imagine, every member of the party set diligently to work to find the missing rubber. Over and over they hunted the miles of glades and mountain sides they had traversed At last they gave it up and returned to the hotel.

But in the afternoon a thought came to Dr. Horton—why not pray that they find the shoe? So he prayed. And they rowed back up the fjord to the landing of the morning, and he got out and walked directly to the overshoe, in a spot he would have sworn he had before searched repeatedly.

I remember a similar experience of my own. There were four of us riding bicycles along a rather sandy road some distance from town. Two were spinning along on a tandem some distance ahead of us, on a down grade, when a rivet flew out and the chain dropped. The tandem ran for a quarter of a mile on down the hill and slowed up on the rise beyond, so that our friends were able to dismount without injury.

By this time we had overtaken them, having ridden in their track, and learned for the first time the cause of their halt. Of course everybody's immediate thought was, "Oh, we can never find that tiny gray rivet in this gray dust—probably the other bicycles ran over it— and home is three miles off." But we all retraced our steps, diligently searching.

Two of the party are crack shots with the rifle, with very quick eyesight. I thought one of these two might find the rivet. But we all walked slowly back, far beyond the point where they became conscious of their loss, and no one spied the rivet.

Then it occurred to me that the high spirit within had not been called to our assistance. Immediately I said to myself, "Spirit, you know where the rivet is!—please show it to me!"

I thought of the spirit as the Law of Love or Attraction, which is the principle of all creation, and instantly the idea came that the little rivet could attract the eye's attention if the eye were willing to be attracted. These words floated into my mind, "Rivet, rivet, rivet my eye!"

By this time I had fallen behind the others. So I walked leisurely, calmly along, eyes willing, and those words saying themselves over and over in my mind.

And the rivet riveted my eye! I, who considered myself very slow of sight, found the rivet. And I know it was because I turned to the universal self, to God, to the Law of Attraction for the help needed, for the knowledge which not one of us had in consciousness, but which was certainly present in the universal mind in which we live and move and have our being.

Just the other day I had a little experience which illustrates the "man's extremity is God's opportunity" idea. For years I have said I could never find ready made garments to fit me. Have tried many times; waists all too short and narrow in front, sleeves skimpy. But I keep trying, every year; for everything is evolving you know, even clothes and tailors.

I wanted a new white lawn shirt waist and wondered if I couldn't find one ready made. I tried the biggest suit house in Springfield; no good.

Then one day I had an impulse to try the best places in Holyoke. I found one or two "almosts," but nothing that would quite do. So I gave it up.

Then I had another impulse to try a store of which I have always said, "I never found there anything I wanted." I nearly passed the store, saying to myself, "No use to try there, and it is late anyway." But there came the thought, or rather impression, that the spirit impelled me and I would better go.

"We'll see if it is the spirit," I said to myself—"I believe it is." It was. I found the [shirt] waist I wanted, and I found a pretty white lawn suit besides! And it was found in the most unlikely corner in the vicinity, according to my judgment and experience.

There is a little law in here that I want you to notice. The spirit leads us through impressions or attractions; and it is limited in its revelations by our mental makeup, which is the conscious and ruling part of us.

Why did not the spirit impress me in the first place to go to that store, where that [shirt] waist and dress had been waiting for me since spring? And I had wanted them since spring. The spirit did impress me about it, but when the spirit said "shirt waist" to me I said, "Springfield—if they haven't a fit there they won't have it anywhere; and anyway I know I'll never find it." But I tried—without faith. That shut the spirit up for the time.

But at the very first opportunity, on the first afternoon when I wasn't too busy to even think about such things, the spirit whispered "shirt waist" to me again. And I didn't let the spirit get any farther with its impressions; instead of asking the spirit where to go for a shirt waist I said, "Oh, yes, shirt waist—of course—I'll go to A.'s and B.'s and C.'s, where I generally get other things that suit me."

You see, my habit mind, preconceived opinions, again settled the matter. It was not until I had given up finding anything at these places, and was going right by the door of the other store, that the spirit had a chance even to whisper its name to me. The spirit had to lead me around all my prejudices in the matter, before it could get me to think of that place.

My mind was open to the thought of the shirt waist, but it was closed hard and fast against the idea of that particular store. At least the direct mental route to that store was closed. So the spirit had to lead me around by back-alley brain connections. But now the direct route is open.

The spirit always goes shopping with me, and nearly always the direct mental routes are open, so I have lots of fun shopping, never waste a lot of time at it, and I nearly always get just what I want, many times at bargain prices, though I almost never look at bargain ads in the papers. But many,

many times have I gone into a store to buy a certain thing and found a big special sale on, of that very item.

Do you think these are very trivial things to be bothering the spirit about? I don't. The spirit is all-wise, all-powerful, everywhere present, and its chief end and joy is to direct folks aright.

The spirit is a sort of universal floor-walker to straighten out the snarls between supply and demand in all departments of life. And I think it is a pretty heedless or foolish individual who won't consult it in every little dilemma.

And I notice that, in spite of this thought, I find myself ignoring the spirit—thinking I know of course where I'd better go for a shirt waist.

It seems hard to remember that Life's store is always growing and changing, so that we can always save time, money and needless meandering, by asking the spirit.

Herein lies the secret of all our little experiences when it looks as if our leading of the spirit was all wrong and our prayers, longing and desires all unanswered: The spirit never fails us. It is we who grow weary following the spirit; which must lead us to the desired goal by way of our own mental paths.

You see, it is a matter of cutting new streets in our mental domain, so it won't be necessary for the spirit to take us by such roundabout ways. It is a matter of clearing out our rocky prejudices so we'll not have to travel around them.

And here the spirit helps us again. As soon as the spirit succeeded in getting me around all my prejudices and into that store I wiped away the prejudice. So there is a straight mental street now where none existed before. The next time the spirit says "shirt waist," to me it can send me straight to D.'s if it wants to.

Yes, the spirit "moves in a mysterious way its wonders to perform." It looks mysterious to us until we are led back by the straight way. Then it is so simple, so easy, we can hardly believe the spirit would condescend to it!

Ah, but it does! Nothing is too small, or too great, for the spirit's attention—if we believe. When we don't believe we are to be pitied—and the spirit keeps discreetly mum.

Chapter IX: Spirit the Breath of Life

"My healer teaches that I must depend alone upon Spirit; that breathing exercises, foods, sunshine and air must not be made the dependence for health. He says, 'Why, you can't help breathing.'"

That is tommyrot. Sunshine and air are spirit, and the plain truth of the matter is that if you don't use them all your "dependence on spirit" will avail simply nothing. Try living in a north room with the windows shut, and see.

You "can't help breathing," but your breathing avails nothing unless by it you take in good fresh live spirit in the way of pure air and sunshine.

If we all lived under the sun and slept under the stars that healer's advice might be good enough. But we don't. We live in tight, dark rooms whence the spirit of life has fled, leaving only its cast off effluvia. We "can't help breathing," but what do we breathe? We breathe the dead air of close rooms.

Spirit is *life*, and we live by breathing it. Spirit is in fresh air; fresh air is in spirit; fresh air and spirit are one. Dead air is air minus spirit, or life.

What good will it do you to say you depend upon spirit when you don't; when you shut yourself away from the spirit of life and breathe death?

Pure air and sunshine are spirit specially prepared for your use. What good will it do you to pretend that you depend upon spirit when you shut yourself into rooms whence the spirit has flown?

If you live in close rooms you may "affirm" your dependence upon spirit until you are black in the face, and you may be "treated" every hour of the day by this healer and 10,000 more like him, and the result will be only sickness and death.

I know in my heart and soul and mind that this is true. And I have seen the truth of it demonstrated by hundreds of cases of people who failed to get well on "treatments" of any sort, and who afterward did get well on sunshine, fresh air and full breathing, along with mental treatment.

The Gospel of Fresh Air is more needed by human beings than even the Gospel of New Thought. If we understood and applied the Gospel of Fresh Air we should think right without trying.

It is in gloomy, unaired corners that evil thoughts breed—because the spirit of life is not present there in such form that it can be appropriated by human beings. They get therein the Breath of Death, and generate thoughts to match—distorted thoughts of death and evil and despair.

Come into the sunshine and breathe the Breath of Life, which generates in you the New Thought of Life, Love, Wisdom, Truth, Health, Happiness, and Success.

New Thought will not save you unless you live it, and a little observation and experimenting will prove to you that you can't live it without breathing plenty of fresh air.

If "all is spirit" why does this healer tell you that to regulate your breathing, exercise, food, etc., is to depend upon something outside spirit?

The fact of the matter is this: He fails to realize that all is spirit. He is still tangled up with good and evil, spirit and not-spirit, God and devil. He does not see spirit in everything and everything in spirit; so he puts the Keep-Off-the-Grass sign wherever he does not see spirit. This will not prevent his pointing you to the spirit where he does recognize it. None of us are wise enough as yet always to see God in all his works.

It is spirit which makes us breathe. When we shut ourselves away from the pure breath of life we shut away the power that makes us breathe.

And when we are too interested in doing indoor work the spirit finds it pretty hard work to make us breathe enough to keep us in good condition for growing. Close rooms and sedentary work defeat the spirit's will to make us breathe.

So we, by working against the spirit, form a habit of breathing too little, thus robbing ourselves of the life, health, wisdom, power, joy which the spirit is trying to give us with every breath.

Now we find ourselves hampered by self-imposed habits which need breaking. So we set ourselves to work with the Spirit of Life. We throw open the window and let in the Spirit of Life.

We go outdoors and revel in the Spirit of Sunshine. We run and jump to make ourselves inbreathe the Spirit of Life.

Being too busy to spend hours every day outdoors we do stunts in our nightdresses to make us inbreathe more of the Spirit of Life.

And always, night and day, winter and summer, we take pains to leave our windows well open that the Spirit of Life be not shut away from us for one single moment.

We are learning to depend wholly upon the Spirit.

We used to remember the Spirit only on the Sabbath day; now we remember it every day and all day and all night—we remember to breathe it and eat it as well as think it.

And verily we are blessed.

Chapter X: Affirmation and Wheels

Mere repetition of "I Am Success" statements will avail little. One must think the thing he desires, and he must put his shoulder to the wheel.

But the person who is full of the sense of failure and defeat is more apt than not to put his shoulder to the wrong side of the wheel. He is so discouraged and preoccupied and worried that he thinks it doesn't matter much where he puts his shoulder, the thing won't budge anyway. So he goes stupidly along drudging away with his shoulder in the same old spot—the wrong spot.

But let that man make up his mind that there is a way to budge that wheel and he will find it; and you will see things move. That man will walk around that wagon a time or two, take in the lay of the land, pat his horses into willing humor, maybe back 'em up a bit, ring out a cheerful "Gid ap," and settle his shoulder to the right spot at the right moment—and away they go. Or another team will pass just at the right time to give him a lift out.

The man who believes himself equal to any emergency which arises will be strong mentally and physically. His mind will be alert, full of expedients. Instead of pushing like a blind mule at one spot until he drops in his tracks, he will use his gumption and find another way. He will conjure up a lever of some sort to budge that load. If he can't do it alone somebody else will come along in the nick o' time to give him the lift he needs. He believes he will work it somehow, and he does.

The "I Am a Failure" man never has anybody come along in the nick o' time. "Just my luck," he whines, and keeps on putting his shoulder to the wrong part of the wheel, or tugging hopelessly and half-heartedly, or—with inward rage that takes more energy than the tug—keeps on until he has to give it up for the time.

To affirm "I Am Success" will not pull the load out of the mire except as it awakes energy to intelligent effort. All affirmations and all going into the silence are useful in waking mental and physical energy to intelligent action.

All chronic failures are such because they believe in failure and opposition and "malicious animal magnetism" and general all-around the-world-is-against-me-ness. This belief in failure fills the individual with an affinity for undesirable things.

The infallible cure, the only cure, for failure, is belief in success, belief in one's own power to turn even defeat to good advantage. The man who "doesn't know when he is beaten" will never be beaten. The "lunkhead" who "didn't know he was a lunkhead" went to the top, while the lunkhead who knew he was a lunkhead stayed at the lunkhead end of the class.

One of our big pork packers once tramped across the continent because he hadn't money to pay his way. After he arrived at his destination he said he saw on his tramp hundreds of places where he could have started in without a cent and in time made piles of money—opportunities just crying to be developed. Only the thought of a bigger chance at the end of the route kept him from stopping in the very first town on his route!

But that boy had success in him and was on the alert for opportunities. He believed in himself and the world. The failure believes only in "bad luck" and his eye is out for "soft snaps," which he is certain he'll never get a chance at.

When a man is looking for trouble and defeat he finds them.

"As a man thinketh in his heart so is he." That does not mean that a man may make a few affirmations of success, or profess new thought, and immediately become a success.

The heart of man is the emotional center of his habits or instinct, the center from which radiate his instincts, his habits, as the nerves radiate from the solar plexus.

Instincts are habit thoughts, heart thoughts. And every instinct came into being through conscious thought and effort.

Follow your internal experiences while learning to play the piano and you will gain a clear idea of how instinct comes into being. At first your fingers are stiff and every movement is a voluntary one, every movement has to be thought about, directed by thought. But gradually you acquire the habit of handling your fingers in a certain way. Gradually you cease to think at all about your finger movements; you "do it instinctively." In other words you have trained your heart, your subconscious mind, to do the thinking for you. Henceforth, instead of thinking consciously about your finger movements you think about them in your heart, that is, sub-consciously.

Psychologists say that not more than five per cent of our mental processes are conscious, the remaining ninety-five per cent being under the consciousness. This means that at least ninety-five per cent of our thoughts are habit thoughts, or "instinctive" thoughts.

It is this instinctive part of us, this ninety-five percent of us, that is referred to in the Bible as "the heart."

Now if this "heart" of us carries at least ninety-five percent of our mentality you can easily see why a man is what he "thinketh in his heart." And you can see why a few affirmations of success, or even a good many of them, will not change the man sufficiently to make any great difference in his surroundings. And you can see why a mere intellectual conception of new thought is not enough to change him and his environment.

Man is a magnet, at least ninety-five per cent of which is habit mind. Therefore by far the greater part of his environment comes to him by its affinity to his ninety-five percent habit or instinct mind, his under-conscious mind, of whose workings he is practically unconscious.

So it is no wonder he so often says, "I don't see why this undesired thing should come to me." He cannot see why it comes, because he is practically unconscious of that great ninety-five per cent of his thinking which draws them. He knows he does not consciously desire these unpleasant things and he can scarcely conceive the fact that he is conscious of only about five per cent of his thoughts and desires.

And, too, he is loath to acknowledge that the greater part of himself has no more sense than to bring such things to him! He feels more complacent when he lays the blame at the door of "environment," or "wicked people," or "malicious animal magnetism," or a "God who chastens whom he loveth," or a devil who got loose from God's leading strings and goes raging about to pester good folks.

Man is a magnet, and every line and dot and detail of his experiences come by his own attraction. "As a man thinketh in his heart so is he." The preponderance of attraction comes through the instinct self, the "heart."

And there is no use in trying to fight off, or run away from, the things which come to us. We only hurt ourselves by fighting. And to run away from the things we have attracted is to run into the arms of similar, or worse, conditions. We have to take ourselves along.

The only way to change conditions effectually is to change "the heart," the habit or instinct mind.

This can be done with more or less ease, according to the degree of setness of character and the degree of will and enthusiasm brought to bear.

The key to all change of character lies with that little five per cent conscious mind, which with all its littleness is a sure lever by which to move the ninety-five percent ponderosity below it. For conscious thought is positive thought, dynamic; while subconscious thought is negative, receptive.

That little five percent mind has stronger compelling power than several times its bulk of sub-conscious mind, and there is not an atom of all that ninety-five per cent subconscious mind which cannot be moved by that little five per cent mind which lies at the top.

The conscious self is the directing power. Just as it directed your fingers to change their fixed habits, so it can direct any change in other lines of mental or bodily habit—by directing persistent, quietly insistent practice on the desired lines.

Insist upon right conscious thinking, and in due time you cannot fail to have right subconscious thinking.

To think good, peace, love, self-command, self-faith, success, long and faithfully enough will fill even the most set "heart" with-habits of good, peace, love, self-command, self-faith, success. And in proportion as the heart becomes filled with such habits the environment and experiences will change to match.

How long will it take thus to transform you by the renewing of your whole mind? All depends upon you. If your practice is fitful and half-hearted it may take another generation or two. If you go at it with a steady will, cutting off all distractions which sap your will and enthusiasm, practicing faithfully and diligently at the new mental habits you may make the desired change in, say, half a lifetime or less.

And if you can bring to your assistance a high spiritual exaltation and faith you can make the change in almost no time at all. For spiritual exaltation and faith and enthusiasm will literally melt the hardest "heart" and permit a quick re-formation.

This is the secret of quick accomplishment in children; their hearts are clean and molten in the emotional fires of enthusiasm and faith, ready to receive deep and lasting impressions.

By [our being schooled in] reason we grown-ups have cooled and even quenched the heart fires of faith and enthusiasm; so it takes time and repetition to re-form us.

This is the secret of miracles. Religious enthusiasm and exaltation are akin to the fires of youth; they melt the heart to receive higher impressions.

The rationalist must receive his new impressions by painstaking hammering in. Repetition and time will do for him what religious or youthful enthusiasm does quickly for babes and fools.

No, affirmations will not do the work of "putting your shoulder to the wheel" when the load is stalled. But they will transform you, heart and consciousness, so that you will attract better horses as well as wheels, better roads, more friends to happen (?) around in the moment of need.

And affirmations of the right sort will wake up your gumption so that you will not overload your horses or your personal energies to the point of needing a shoulder at the wheel.

Success is the natural result of intelligent direction of effort.

Affirmations of success, faith, wisdom, power, good, love, will wake your latent forces to more intelligent uses.

The more enthusiasm you can conjure into the affirmations the more quickly will you realize success.

Chapter XI: Your Forces and How to Manage Them

You can overdo anything, even self-treatment. If you keep repeating affirmations to yourself your mental chattering interferes with the real healing.

It is not the conscious mind which heals you; it is the subconscious or soul mind and the super-conscious or Over-Soul mind.

Your soul's expression is guided and directed by your conscious mind. A mental affirmation is simply a word of direction to your soul mind. The soul hears your statements and then builds accordingly.

But what would happen if you called up your housemaids and told them over and over, just what you wanted done and just how to do it? If you spent all your time repeating your directions to them when would they get the work done? And wouldn't they get your directions mixed, too? Of course.

You don't do it that way, of course not; not if you are a wise housekeeper. You call up your maids and tell them quietly and kindly, and in as few words as possible, just what you want done. Then they go cheerfully away out of your presence and do their best to please you. If you later come across something which was not done right you call in a maid and repeat your directions, with perhaps a little further explanation. Then you go away again and trust her to do it aright this time.

What would happen if you tagged around after your maids and tried to watch and criticize and direct every little movement? Why, they would grow nervous and make foolish mistakes and you would all give up in despair.

And what would happen if you directed them to do a certain difficult piece of work and then came back five minutes later expecting to find it all done? Oh, you can't imagine yourself doing such foolish things!

Perhaps you don't with your maids, but evidently you do with your own self. Your objective, everyday consciousness is the mistress or master of your being.

Psychologists say the objective mental activities are not more than one twentieth of all your mental activities. That means that the mistress mind has the equivalent of at least twenty maids under her direction. These "maids" belong to the subjective mind, or soul of you.

Then there is the great Over-Soul, of which your individual soul is but an atom; but an atom whose every demand is heard. That means that your little mistress mind not only has at her bidding the equivalent of at least twenty maids of the subconscious, but she has also at her call the equivalent of ten million billion other helpers of the infinite Over-Soul.

And all the mistress mind has to do is say the word. All these helpers fly to do her bidding.

Perhaps you think all these helpers don't fly to do your bidding. But they do. The only trouble with you is that you don't give your helpers time and chance to work out your desires. You keep repeating your directions over and over, and you keep trying to tag around after all your twenty or more housemaids to see if they are doing the things you want done. You watch them in your stomach and your liver and your lungs, always fretting for fear they are going wrong.

No wonder you get nervous and fidgety and strained all over; no wonder your "feelings" are no better than they were!

Make your statements of health, happiness and success at certain regular intervals, say two or three times a day. Or make them at times when you can't get your mind off your conditions.

Make the statements plainly and positively. Then call your mind entirely away from the subject and give your soul and the Over-Soul a chance to work. Make light of your feelings and go get well interested in some good work.

Take it for granted that all your being, and all creation besides, is working out for you the things you desire. Rest easy and trust yourself.

Don't let your mind tag your feelings and symptoms; give it plenty of useful work and plenty of play and plenty of rest while your soul works things out for you as fast as it can. Just be as interested and happy as you can while the soul is working. Jolly yourself into having a good time.

Say the Word, and then be happy and do not allow yourself to doubt that the soul will do the work. This is the secret of quick healing. The nearer you can come to keeping your mind pleasantly occupied between the times when you give yourself special affirmations and treatments, the more quickly you will realize health of mind, body and environment as well as soul.

Thy faith in thy soul and the Over-Soul will have made thee whole.

The faithless mind is a terrible meddler and creator of discords; and the idle mind, the mind not directed to useful purposes, is always a faithless meddler.

Moral: Get interested in some good work.

Chapter XII: Duty and Love

Though you work your fingers to the bone and have not love for your work it profits you next to nothing and your employer less than it ought to.

Duty work robs the doer of the joy of doing, which is the chief compensation for all work.

You imagine you do your work well from a sense of duty. You would do it better still if you loved it. If you loved it you would enjoy every bit of it, and you would glory in every little improvement you hit upon; and you would hit upon a lot because your soul would be playing through your fingers.

The soul of the duty doer is shut away from his work—he works with his fingers and his habit mind only. By the end of the week he is fagged out and his poor soul droops for lack of exercise; then perhaps he takes it to church for relief; and shuts it carefully away again before Monday morning.

And the worst of it is that so many people make a virtue of keeping their souls locked up six days out of seven. They parade duty as their mainspring. And even when they do happen to let a little soul, a little love and joy into their work they won't acknowledge it. They stick to it that it is "duty" which impels them.

When the soul does manage to get out of its shell and express itself in useful work the brain denies it the glory and happiness which belong to it. The worker resolutely shuts off the joy vibrations with that stem word "duty." He robs himself of the pleasure of his honest effort.

There are two ways of robbing one's self of the joy of work. One is by paralyzing joy with "duty"; the other is by scattering the mind and soul all over creation whilst the hands are doing something. In the former case the soul is shut away in idleness; in the latter it is wasted in riotous thinking.

The soul's power is emotion, that which flows from the silence within. The nature of emotion is motion. To let emotion move through the body, out into intelligent effort, is joy and eternally welling life and strength and wisdom.

To let the mind wander while the hands work is to fritter your soul force away at the top of the head—the power which should move from the head down through the body and out into intelligent doing, is simply dissipated into thin air.

The wandering mind robs the body of vitality and joy. It is the prodigal who wastes all your substance.

The duty doer is a niggard. He lets some of his soul into his work, shutting the rest tight within. He puts his thought into his work, but he is stingy with his soul, his love. He works coldly, stolidly, conscientiously, reminding himself constantly that he is to "be good for nothing," as the wise mamma commanded the little boy who wanted a prize for being good.

Now everybody knows that cold contracts things. The cold duty doer shuts off his soul warmth and his body grows gaunt and pinched, his brain cells stiff, his thoughts angular. He shuts off the inspiration of love and joy and works like a machine, grinding out the same old things by the same old pattern.

The duty doer converts a real living, growing, loving being into a mere cold machine. It's a shame. And the whole cause is the old fathers' tradition that duty is greater than love. I wonder where they got that notion?

The same spirit led them that leads us. That same spirit must have led them and us into duty doing.

Why? To gain self-control that we might have the greater joy. That is it! First there is the "natural," the animal way of doing things; just to follow impulse and gratify self at no matter what expense to others. But somehow you are not very happy after you have done it.

Then there is the mental way of doing things, the "duty" way; when we cut off all the old "natural" impulses and teach ourselves to work stolidly, steadily in the "right" line.

It takes about all our thought and effort to control ourselves in this mental way; it requires a firm unrelenting hand upon our impulses. But we were not happy when we didn't control our impulses, and we are at least at peace when we do. So we keep on crushing back the "natural" impulses and sticking sternly to duty.

When we followed the old animal impulses to have things our way right or wrong, without regard to the other fellow, we were always lured on by the hope of joy; and when we got the thing desired, as we sometimes did, it was only to be disappointed. So we were full of unrest. Since we have chosen the ways of duty there are no joys to lure us, but rest accompanies us.

In the old way we were always sure we were going to be happy; in the duty way we have ceased to expect happiness but we really have peace. And a peace in the heart, we have learned from sad experience, is worth two joys in the bush. We have been oft bitten and thus learned caution: so we keep on schooling ourselves to keep the peace and shut eyes and ears to promises of pleasure.

We have learned to follow "conscience" instead of "natural impulse." Conscience is merely spiritual caution. The faculty called caution warns us from outward danger; it was created by many ages of race experience in getting its fingers burned and its shins kicked and its head broken Conscience warns us from inner dangers; and is being created by many ages of human experience at stealing from the other fellow only to find its own heart robbed of peace and happiness.

We tasted impulse and found it sweet at first and bitter, bitter at the last. Then we tasted duty and found its first pungency melt away to a clean sweetness such as we had never tasted before; a sweetness so pure and satisfying that it is no wonder we keep clinging to the duty doing which brought it.

When we lived from unchecked and unguided impulse only we were many times happy on the surface, when we happened to get the things asked for, but we were always restless and dissatisfied within. This unrest is the voice of the universal spirit within, which is ever urging us to take our dominion over self and to direct our energies to higher and yet higher uses; it is the voice of life, which ever demands a high purpose for being and doing.

The spirit of the world which is moving us allows each a few years and many intervals of irresponsible living. We have our childhood when the whole world smiles and flies to gratify every impulse; and when we are good children we have our little vacations and play happily with that sweet taste in our hearts. If we try to take too many play times the spirit in us is frowning and restless again, ever urging us to be up and doing that which will help the world spirit express the beauties it has in mind for us.

When we quit chasing pleasure and begin to live and do after the plan set in our hearts the world spirit whispers "Well done," to us. We find peace. We taste and see that it is good. Henceforth we work for the inner peace, not for the fleeting gratification of the outer senses.

As we follow duty peace deepens and widens. By and by we form the habit of duty and it grows easier and easier. We do what seems best because we have learned that to do otherwise ruffles our peace; and we have learned to love that peace beyond anything else life can hold for us.

Peace keeps on deepening and widening and growing more dynamic. At first it is a solemn calm, and a little deviation from duty ruffles and dissipates it. But by and by as we keep on doing our duty, through this solemn calm, growing ever deeper and broader, there wells the full diapason of a deep joy—very softly at first, with many diminuendos and silences; at unexpected moments it swells again; over little things the tide of life has brought us—things we loved, and thought we had given up forever when we chose duty as our guide.

Fitfully at first the deep joy wells, fitfully and gently, but, oh, so full and sweet and satisfying; such tones as our souls never heard before. We wonder at the deep joy; and, oh, we begin to see that the world spirit was urging us on to duty only that we might find deeper joy than the old irresponsible life could yield us. By taking dominion over self, by using our energies for higher purposes, we have deepened our capacity for joy.

Now the harmony of deep joy begins to swell, and every touch of life but adds to the paeans of praise.

And the good things of life begin to come—houses, lands, fathers, mothers, brothers, a hundredfold more than ever before, bringing joy such as we never knew before. Oh, we thought we had given up the pleasures of life for its duties, and behold we find the pleasures added.

We used to be fascinated and tossed about by life's pleasures; now we find them fascinated and obedient to us—oh, the power and glory and joy of it!

We gained dominion over ourselves and our environment through doing our duty. We gave up the shortsighted impulse "will" to follow the omniscient will which is working through us, and behold the things we once desired vainly are now ours to command and enjoy. No wonder we laud duty!

But duty is a schoolmaster whose work we do not need forever. When we have made its wisdom our own, we outgrow duty. Duty flowers in love.

The more resolution and persistence we put into duty doing the sooner we shall outgrow it.

The more pleasure we can get out of duty doing the faster we shall outgrow it. When the worker puts his soul into his duty, duty is swallowed up in love, and joy grows.

Many a duty worker cheats himself out of the joy which is his, and stunts the growth of his joy and himself, simply by denying that he works from anything but a sense of duty.

As long as our best efforts are called duty they answer to the call as cold, hard duty.

As soon as those same activities are called pleasures, our soul joy and love, are turned into them and they are transfigured.

The worker who calls his work duty shuts his soul back from his body and his work. The soul of you is love, and love has no affinity for duty; so as long as you insist upon working from a sense of duty you shut in, shut away from your work, the sense of love. You thus rob yourself of the joy of doing.

And this means that you rob yourself of the greater share of your power and wisdom for doing.

Love is the essence of all wisdom, imagination and inspiration, as well as power. To hold sternly to duty is to shut out love, and with it the wisdom, inspiration and imagination necessary to improve your work. You are robbed of the joy of doing, and your work is robbed of its highest beauty and usefulness.

Quit calling your duties by that name. Jolly yourself into doing your duty for love of it. Don't you know how you can jolly a child into doing things? Haven't you been jollied yourself until at last you laughed and forgave and did the thing you had sternly resolved not to do? Haven't you seen scores of your friends jollied into doing things? Of course. All nature responds to a smiling good-willed jolly.

And your soul, your love, will respond to the same good-willed jollying. It will come out and smile on your doings, and radiate soul-shine and joy and power and inspiration through you, and down through your fingers into your work, and out into your aura, and on out to all the world.

Smile and come up higher than the duty class—the *joy* class awaits you!

Chapter XIII: Well Done

"Natural disaster overtakes a man and he loses every cent. Possessing untold aversion to becoming a paid employee, he lives with friends, helping where able, and at the same time reaching out to grasp something by which to start again. Has an overwhelming desire to get money for home and marriage. This could be had in a very short time by successful speculation, if the unlimited Force is there as taught, for use on lines of desire. There is no wrong in the world. Is he then to command the powers for conscious use, go in faith and win; or shall he sit down and build, bit by bit, by uncongenial labor?" —M.T.

The man who possesses such "an untold aversion to becoming a paid employee" that he prefers to sponge a living off his friends rather than to earn it honestly, will never succeed even at speculation.

Such a man could not generate a desire strong enough to attract fortune even at a gambling table.

It takes character to generate a desire of the sort that moves things. It takes steadiness of purpose, positive determination.

And character, purpose, determination, are never found in the sponger.

If he had character he would choose any sort of honest work that would keep him in independence. His "untold aversion to becoming a paid employee" would be as nothing to his disgust for sponging a living, even temporarily.

Character is the outcome of an unconquerable self-respect and self-reliance. A man's character is that which distinguishes him from a jellyfish, which takes the shape of any environment that happens along. It is Something which keeps him upright on his own pins, no matter what happens.

Character is mental backbone and muscle, and is subject to the same laws of development and growth as other bone and muscle.

Bone and muscle and character do not grow by bread alone, but by use. Character grows by the use of self-reliance and self-respect, just as physical character grows by the use of muscles. Character becomes weak and flabby when self-reliance and self-respect are kept on the shelf of another man's pantry.

Character develops by exercise. How is it to exercise except by doing things? How is it to do things when somebody else does them for him?

The first thing a man of character, of self-respect and self-reliance would do under such circumstances as M.T. describes would he to overcome his "untold aversion" to anything which would help him to continue living in self-respect and self-reliance. Indeed the only "untold aversion" held by a man of real character is the "untold aversion" to living off other people.

A person whose aversion to "becoming a paid employee" is greater than his aversion to idleness and sponging is a mere mush of concession to public opinion—he hates paid employment because he thinks his neighbors will "look down" upon him, and because he likes to look aristocratic and give orders rather than to be what he is and take what orders are necessary for the time being.

Such a man cares for appearances above all things. He cares for the outside of things, as a jellyfish does. He seeks first an agreeable resting place, as the Jellyfish does. And he will sacrifice the last vestige of self-respect, self-reliance, character, to that fetish, outside appearance. He thinks it looks better to live off his friends than to soil his hands to take care of himself.

But if he had a real character of his own, if he had mental backbone and muscle worthy the name, he simply could not crouch and cringe as a dependent, a beggar. He would have to get out and express himself in some sort of independent activity, or die.

For character is a deep-down life-urge which will push to expression through any conditions. It simply cannot continue to sit supinely by another man's fireside, or wait by the wayside with cap extended to catch stray pennies from the passers-by.

Character must act, or degenerate.

Character must ex-press, or ex-pire.

Character is to the individual what the channel is to the river. Take away the banks which confine the stream and direct it, and the water gushes out in an endless sloppy marsh.

The inner character of a man confines and directs the life force, the desire force.

The stronger the character the deeper and broader the stream of desire, or life; and the more positively the man will express himself in independent, self-respecting activity.

The stronger the character the greater will be the man's "untold aversion" to depending upon anybody but himself.

And so deep and strong are his desires as they flow through the clear-cut channels of character, that they force new channels through any circumstances. Such a man's desires flow deep and strong enough to carry things his way.

But the man without a strong character is a mere sloppy marsh of sentimentality. He is incapable of anything more than "overwhelming desires"—his desire stream, having no strong banks, simply overwhelms the whole surface of things, with no depth by which to sweep its way through environment. His desire energy spreads out and wastes itself in mere shallow longings, unworthy the name of desire. So the man welters in his own swamp of sensibility, and gets nowhere.

Herein lies the reason that M.T.'s man will not find success at the gaming table, nor anywhere else, except by "building bit by bit" a character strong enough to find its way to the good things he wants.

The first step toward success is to decide that it is yours, and that all creation is ready to help you manifest it.

The next step is to work with the world, taking hold anywhere that the world will let you, in full confidence that the world will promote you as fast as you prove your fitness for promotion.

To prove your fitness for promotion necessitates doing your best with any job the world gives you, and at the same time using your spare time and thought in fitting yourself for a better one.

To do one of these things is not enough. The man who does his work exceptionally well will be kept at that same kind of work until crack o' doom unless he shows aptitude for doing more valuable work. The world is always looking eagerly for men who can fill the more difficult positions. It is always trying to tempt people into higher, better paying positions; and the man who is faithful and efficient in one place, and evinces the slightest capacity for higher work, is always the first man to get a chance of promotion.

The man who thinks he is "kept down" is right; but he is kept down by himself alone. Either he is slack, inefficient, uninterested, gumptionless in his present work; or he is not fitting himself for something better.

Abe Lincoln split rails all day. He split them with vim and intelligence. But at night he studied books by the light of a pine knot. All the way along from rail splitting to the presidency, Abe found some time out of business hours to inform himself on lines beyond his work.

The main difference between Abe Lincoln and Abe Johnson lies in the way they spend their after-business hours. Abe Johnson, too, works with vim and intelligence. And he never had to split rails for a living. He is an A-1 bookkeeper. Been in the same store, with almost the same salary, for twenty-five years. And almost every noon and every evening for twenty-five years he has sat on a sugar keg in the store and discussed politics and economics. And very often he has grumbled to his cronies about his lack of a chance to rise in the world.

Down here in a Massachusetts town, they have been having labor troubles for a long time. The cotton mill owners say the bottom has dropped out of the plain cotton cloth trade and they simply must reduce wages or close down. There is small demand for the sort of plain cotton goods manufactured in these mills. The mill hands say they can't live on any smaller wages and they won't, so there. So one strike follows another, or a lockout. For months at a time the mills lie idle while owners and workers deadlock.

Some one suggested that the mills begin to make the sort of new fancy weaves of cotton cloth for which there is increasing demand. But the weavers refused to learn the new weaves. They said they knew how to do the plain weaving and it "wouldn't pay them" to learn the new kind of weaving on the old wages, which are paid according to the amount of work done. And many of them said anyway they were too old to make such changes now.

So these faithful and efficient weavers go on fighting and striking and reviling "fate" rather than fit themselves for new work which would in the end pay better than the old.

Poor shortsighted weavers.

Poor shortsighted cousins to the weavers.

Poor shortsighted and disappointed Abe Johnson.

What do you suppose life makes us begin at the bottom for, and "build bit by bit"? For the sole purpose of building character; building good, strong channels for desire to run in; channels so deep and full that the desire-stream will be strong enough to accomplish for the individual the thing he wants.

And how are we to know we are building the right kind of character? By the sense of inner satisfaction which witnesses every well-done deed.

That is where self-respect and self-reliance come in. Even a baby feels the "Well done" of its soul when it succeeds in doing something for itself. A child prizes this inner self-satisfaction, self-respect, above all things else. Watch the happy look on a child's face when it has succeeded in doing something for itself.

Only foolish grown-ups value anything on earth above this inner satisfaction. Only grown-ups will let other folks do for them what they can do for themselves. Only grown-ups will quench themselves for the sake of appearances. Some "grown-ups."

To know thyself is to know that the best thing in heaven or earth, the best guide in heaven or earth, is the inner sense of "Well done," the sense of self-respect which comes from doing things instead of letting them be done for you.

As long as the innermost self approves your doings you are building character. And what shall it profit you if you gain the whole world and lose the "Well done" of your soul?

Nothing! Less than nothing!

For in all creation or uncreation there is but one real satisfaction, one real happiness, and that is self-satisfaction, self-respect.

Self-respect springs only from well-doing. It is "Well done," thy soul says to thee, that gives thee joy.

What matter what Tom, Dick, and Harry and Madame Grundy say? Be still and hear thyself.

Eye hath not seen nor ear heard the glory and satisfaction which await him who listens to himself.

"Well done, good and faithful servant; enter thou into the joy of thy Lord"—which is thy innermost self.

Chapter XIV: What Has He Done?

We were talking about new thought and the increased efficiency it gives to people. Evidently he did not think very highly of the practical side of new thought. It is all very well to help people to bear their troubles, he said, but it does not get rid of the troubles.

And I said I thought if it never did anything more than help people to endure things, it at least helps more than anything else ever did.

But I assured him that new thought rightly applied does change conditions, and I cited my own experience in proof. Then I called his attention to other people, prominent in the new thought, whose conditions and health have been changed for good. One of the names mentioned was that of a successful lawyer well known to us both. "Well," queried he, "what has he done that is so wonderful? Others have done as great or greater things, who never heard of new thought."

Of course. The principles of new thought are the principles of life itself, and in all climes and times there have been people who, consciously or unconsciously, lived according to principle and thereby manifested health (which means wholeness) of mind, body and environment.

Wisdom's ways are always ways of pleasantness and all her paths are peace.

And wisdom is as omnipresent as the ethers, to be used by him who inspires it—by him who desires it above all else.

Every pleasant thing and thought in this world comes by mental breathing of wisdom. And every soul that ever lived has lived by breathing wisdom.

In proportion to his inbreathing of wisdom has been the pleasantness of his ways and the peace of his path.

And his ups and downs have come from the fact that he inspires wisdom in spots only. He keeps on mentally breathing, of course; but he doesn't always breathe wisdom. He is like a man who breathes pure outdoor air awhile, and then goes into a close room, or down in a mine, and breathes poison gases.

As physical health depends upon the quantity of pure air inspired, so physical and mental and environmental health depends upon the amount of pure wisdom inspired.

And nobody will deny that most of us inspire a large proportion of poison gas of the mental kind, instead of pure wisdom. We breathe over other people's thoughts after them, just as we breathe over the air after them. This breathed-over thought destroys our physical, mental and environmental health. We need to get out in God's open air and breathe new thought, or we shall asphyxiate.

Old thought is division, dissension, separateness, competition.

New thought is the great opening of principles, oneness, harmony, God, good, freedom, peace, love.

New thought is from ages to ages everlasting. Those who inspire it, inbreathe it, are the whole and strong ones, whether they breathe it consciously or unconsciously.

By teachings of new thought the world is learning to do consciously, intelligently, what a few have done here and there through all the ages. And need we be reminded of the advantages of knowing how and why we do things?

"What has he done that is so wonderful?" The lawyer we spoke of is not what the world calls "great" in any line. He has not built up a Standard Oil "system," nor torn one down. He is not a Roosevelt or a Togo, or a Napoleon, nor even an Elbert Hubbard. His desires and ambitions have run in other lines. He is not "built that way." He "hasn't it in him" to be a Rockefeller, and he is glad of it.

Why then should he be compared with Napoleon or Rockefeller? Do we measure roses and violets and daffodils and chrysanthemums by the same standards? Is the violet inconsequential because it sheds its sweetness in a shady comer instead of flinging it in midday from the top of a sunflower stalk? No. We measure violets by other violets, not by sunflowers or hollyhocks or peonies.

And men are more diverse than flowers. Every man has his own individuality, his own soul specifications to develop by. Every man comes as the flower of a peculiar ancestry, like no other man's ancestry. To judge one man by another is as foolish as to judge a violet by a sunflower.

This lawyer we spoke of stands in a class by himself. He has not achieved what Rockefeller has, but he has achieved something which satisfies himself better than the doings of a dozen Standard Oil magnates could.

And what is success but self-satisfaction?

To succeed is to accomplish what one sets out to do.

A growing success is a matter of growing ideals and a succession of successes.

Our lawyer is satisfied with new thought and its efficacy in his case. By its use he has accomplished a succession of things he wanted to do. He has literally made himself over, and his environment, too. And he has evolved new ideals and developed new energies which show him a joy-full eternity ahead.

He is satisfied with the new thought as a working principle.

He goes on working by it, growing daily in wisdom and knowledge, daily growing greater graces of character, mind, body and environment.

It is the man who does not live new thought teachings who misjudges them by the outward appearances of other men's lives.

Chapter XV: Will and Wills

Nothing before, nothing behind;
  The Steps of faith
Fall on the seeming void, and find
  The Rock beneath.
    —Whittier

In a copy of an old magazine is an article entitled, "What New Thought Women Say of the Will, by an Old Thought Woman," who fails to sign her name. This article is about as cross-eyed as anything I have read recently. It amuses me. And yet it touches a responsive chord of stored memories, and I sympathize.

That is, I am enabled for the moment to re-enter the same-pathy or condition this woman describes Every step she has passed through I, too, have experienced.

But I have passed through it all and emerged upon the spiral above, where I am enabled to understand the phenomena of wills in relation to each other, and in relation to the whole.

Briefly stated, "The Old Thought Woman's" idea is, "The will is a part of that delusive mortal mind. It is the executor of the world, the flesh and the Devil. 'God's will' is a fiction." "Devil" with a capital D, mind you. Then she goes on to tell how willful she used to be; she dominated her relatives, friends and enemies alike, and even the cats and dogs. "There was scarcely no way in which will can dominate that I did not work to its limits," she says; "I intended to marry without declaring my views, get the property and support, but refuse all sensuality," because she was "adamant against child-bearing."

Decidedly a disagreeable person, I should say. I don't wonder that she was "cordially hated by those whom she hypnotized and outwitted"; I don't wonder "pain, anguish, hatred, suffering, disappointment followed in the wake of every triumph." Do you?

Then she grew sick of it all and "gave up all will." "In a complete loss of will, self-will, God's will, all kinds of will, there is a miraculous condition of affairs," she says. Then she goes on to preach Christ's teaching of non-resistance.

Every positive character, and probably every negative one, too, passes sometime through an experience identical with this woman's. The more pronounced the character the more definite is the change from self-will to self-abnegation.

A negative character will hang on eternally to his self-will, and the giving up of his will causes him all the anguish this woman experienced as a result of using her will.

Now without pointing out to you the mistakes of this writer let me give you my statement of will, its nature and uses; after which I think you will see the Old Thought Woman's understanding needs to grow a bit.

Will is the motive, electric force of the universe; the only force there is.

Will is the energy which forms worlds and swings them in space; which dissolves all forms and creates anew.

Will is attraction and gravitation.

Will is love, and will is hate.

Will is the passion, the active force, of the One.

Will is omnipresent and omnipotent.

Without will there could be only stagnation, death, annihilation.

But there is Will; and there are wills; there is all-pervading, all-evolving Will, and there are countless little tossing, warring wills. There is one great ocean, and there are countless little, tossing wavelets, each taken up with its own aims to rise above its neighbors.

On the unseen side Will is one, the only One. On the seen side there are only wills, beginning and ending within the personal circle.

Will is the executive of omniscience.

Will is the executive of universal, all-evolving Wisdom. "Will of God" is no fiction; it is the one immutable, inexorable *fact* which personal wills ceaselessly and uselessly toss themselves against, to their undoing and the increase of knowledge.

All-Wisdom and All-Will are the one great ocean, from which personal wisdom and will are tossed, and to which all return.

Will and Wisdom are all there is in the universe; they are one and inseparable. Water is correctly formulated as W2W, instead of H_2O; and every atom in the universe, seen or unseen, is simply Will in definite and varying proportion to Wisdom. The less Wisdom in the mixture the more foolishly will the Will be exercised.

Will is used commonly as a name for volition exercised by the conscious 5 per cent mind. The individual reasons from his own narrow view and sets his will to execute his finite judgments.

For the time, he sets his judgment up as infallible, grits his teeth, clinches his fists and drives through;—until he comes slam up against Universal Will.

It is as if one of your hands set up a judgment of its own and attempted to force the other hand to move after his pattern. Your right hand sees and judges for a right hand, but not for a left hand.

Just so with this Old Thought Woman; she set up her judgment and attempted to bring relatives, friends, enemies, animals, under subjection.

Under subjection to what?—her will? No—under subjection to her judgments. Her will was simply the executive—the sheriff's posse. Having a strong will she had her way in many cases, where a less determined individual would have held just as severe judgments without having the will to execute them.

Was her will "evil," a "delusion"? No. But her wisdom was a minus, a personal, quantity and her will thereby misdirected.

I am a very strong willed woman and I glory in it. But the time was when I made all kinds of a chump of myself by setting up my judgment for other people's guidance, and sending my will to execute my judgments, willy-nilly on the other fellow's part.

My will was first class; likewise my intention; but my judgment was exceedingly narrow and crude. I got into all kinds of hot water, just as this Old Thought Woman did; and finally I couldn't stand it any longer.

I "went to the Lord." I prayed and agonized and humbled myself—as I needed to. The trouble with me was that I had not learned yet that my judgments were not the best on earth and my will [was not] the only executive.

All these failures on my part made me look at last for higher judgments and mightier will.

Among men I could not find them. Not a writer or lecturer or friend but showed me plainly that his judgments were as wry and his will as circumscribed as my own. So I turned to the unseen and unbelieved-in, but greatly needed and longed for God. I "gave up my will"—I said, "Not my will but thine be done."

It was hard to do, but being a strong willed woman I did it and did it well. I lived daily with Jesus in that sublime "Sermon on the Mount."

Of course "I found peace." Having laid aside all personal aims and ambitions and given up all efforts to make myself or the world better, I found peace.

An Indian lying full length in his canoe, which is floating softly and surely down the broad Columbia toward the ocean, is an emblem of peace.

The individual who wakes up at last to the fact that what he has been tearing himself in tatters trying to accomplish is already being accomplished by a broad river of Will of which his own will is but a wavelet, finds himself embodying peace.

"He that loseth his life shall find it." He that loseth his will shall find it—for the first time.

I thought I was giving up my will, when it was only my judgments I gave up. And I gained in return the entire will of the universe. I changed my point of view—that was all.

I had been seeing countless myriads of striving, tortured individuals, each warring in chaos to bring order according to his judgments.

Now I saw God as the animating soul and will and wisdom working in and through and by these striving ones.

From a formless wavelet striving to get up, I became the Indian, resting, realizing the mighty Will underneath me that carried me unerringly in the right direction even when I did nothing.

I rested and let the All-Will carry me and everybody else. At times it seemed that I must spring up and make this one or that one go right or do right. But I used my will on myself and kept hands off.

I could not see that the All-Will was bringing this out right; but I had made such a miserable failure when I was running things that in sheer despair I determined to resist nothing, compel nobody, but just trust that the All-Will would bring things out right.

I kept saying to myself, "Hands off—hands off;—loose him and let the All-Will run him," until I really learned to let the All-Will do it.

Of course I thought, just as this Old Thought Woman does, that I was exercising no will at all. But I was, and she is doing it, too.

The only difference between the use of my will before and after this self-abnegation was this: After I "gave up my will" I had the All-Will on my side for the first time, and so easy did it seem to be to let the All-Will do everything, that I did not realize that the All-Will worked through and by my personal will.

It was as if I had been trying desperately to lift something too heavy for me, and suddenly my efforts were reinforced to such an extent that it was easy. Or, as if I had been trying hard to shove open what seemed a door when along came one who showed me where the real door was and how to open it easily.

I had been using all my will to make myself and others "good" and suddenly I found the All-Will reinforcing my little will—as if a mighty power had been switched on to my circuit.

This was not really what happened, you know. It was this: My little will had been striving against other little wills—as if one finger strove to curtail the action of another finger. At last, in desperation and without at the time understanding what I did—I let go my little attempt; and immediately I began to sense the All-Will working through my will for the accomplishment of larger purposes I had not before dreamed of.

It was hard to strive against other wills—hard; and the outcome uncertain, and fraught with suffering and disappointment. But it was easy to let the All-Will back my will—so easy I failed for some time to realize I was using any will.

Like Solomon I asked for wisdom, for understanding. As it came to me I saw that whenever the All-Will backed my will and made action easy I was on the right track; whenever I felt a sensation of pulling against some other will I was on the wrong track and must let go and rest.

Many times the thing I could not at one time do without that pulling against feeling, at another time I could do easily with that sense that the All-Will backed me. Sometimes the All-Will backed me in doing what some other person opposed, and yet I was not backed when I did the opposing.

At first all this seemed like the capricious "leadings" of a "spirit." But at last I began to see a principle in it.

I found the Law of Individuality. I found that when I willed to do anything which I desired, the All-Will backed me, unless I foolishly desired to curtail what some other body desired to do—not what some other body desired me to do, but what he desired to do without interference from me. Do you see the point?

For instance, I desired to teach and heal; another desired me to cook and sew; and the spirit backed me. I serenely taught and healed. That other fumed and fretted, and yet, all serene, I knew the All-Will backed me. But that other smoked; I considered smoking wasteful and detrimental; and every time I expressed my opinions on the subject I felt that the All-Will was not backing me.

This one had a right to smoke, because he was not thereby interfering with the free action of another. But when he tried to put me back in the kitchen he had to use his personal will un-backed by the All-Will; because the All-Will was backing my will to get out of the kitchen. On the other hand, the All-Will backed his will to smoke; therefore, when I tried to interfere I opposed not only his will but the All-Will as well.

Now that is just what gives us all so many hard knocks in the world, dearie. We fail to respect the other fellow's rights, and in so doing we run against not only his personal will but the All-Will into the bargain. No wonder we get some horrible bumps.

When you exercise your will against another's freedom of action you shut yourself off from your source of will supply, the All-Will. This is why you clinch your fists, grit your teeth and contract your lungs and muscles. You are shut off from the source of will supply, and you contract in order to force your will power against another. Then you are exhausted, and have accomplished nothing. For if you succeed in "making him be good" this time he hates you for it. And he will break out with more force at the next opportunity—because the All-Will is backing him even in the actions you judge as "bad."

Remember, the All-Will backs every personal will except when the personal will interferes with the free action (not interference) of another will.

Then, when you attempt interfering with the free action of another you force out your will upon him, just as you force out the breath from your lungs. Then you have to "catch your breath" and your will again.

It takes time to fill yourself again with will, and whilst you are doing it you suffer all those horrible sensations of remorse and weakness and disgust that come over one after one of these tussles with another will. You have all these feelings whether or not you succeed in downing the other fellow.

Oh, it doesn't pay, dearie. It doesn't pay to use your will except when you can feel the All-Will backing you.

What new thought people refer to as "cultivating the Will" is simply cultivating acquaintance with and consciousness of the All-Will. It is simply recognition of will; recognition of the ceaseless, underlying urge of the uni-verse which is working within and through the individual to express more and more of beauty and wisdom and good.

To use the little, personal will apart from the All-Will one must contract and thus force out his will upon other people and things.

To use the All-Will one must first know he is right, then relax and let will flow through him to accomplish according to his word or desire.

In using the little, personal will one recognizes himself a member of a "multi-verse"—a being separate and apart from all other beings.

In order to use the All-Will one must first have learned his relation to it and to all other persons and things; he must have recognized the uni-verse, and himself and others as orderly, useful members of the uni-verse.

Only as he recognizes Oneness is it possible for him to resign the exercise of the small, personal will and let the All-Will accomplish through himself and through every other man.

He that loseth his will shall find it one with All-Will.

And after all it is not his will he has lost, but his beliefs about it and its use. He has come up higher and caught a glimpse of the unity of things. He has hitched his wagon to omnipotence and behold all things are done according to his word.

The All-Will backs the individual in anything good, bad or indifferent, which he wills to do; just so long as the individual does not interfere with other individuals.

So you see, in any effort you may make toward self-development you have All-Will working with and through you. And if you will attend strictly to business nothing on earth or in hell can stem the tide of your will, and so defeat you.

"There is no chance, no destiny, no fate, Can circumvent or hinder or control,

The firm resolve of a determined soul."

Chapter XVI: Concerning Vibrations

Vibration is Life. Vibration is motion. All motion is vibration. All motion is Life. You expand your chest with an inhalation of air; you contract your muscles and exhale. This is vibration. Your heart "beats." This, too, is vibration.

Every tiny cell in your body is "beating," or vibrating, just as your heart and lungs do.

When your chest expands you take in fresh air, which goes not only into your lungs, but into all parts of your body. The air blows like a fresh breeze around the countless millions of cells which go to make up your body. These little cells in their turn expand and take in the air. Then the cells contract and force out the air, and your lungs, too, contract, and force the air clear out of your body.

Now this air which is thus vibrated through your body serves to clean it. The decaying particles of your body cells are thrown off and carried out in the streams of air which are vibrated through your body. If it were not for this vibration of your body, which keeps the air flowing through, your body would soon become clogged with dead matter.

The nerves and arteries in your body are constantly contracting and expanding, contracting and expanding, to move along the blood, which carries food supply to the cells and bears away their sewage in just the same way that the air is carried to and from the cells.

It is by constantly vibrating—contracting and expanding—that your stomach and bowels digest food.

It is by vibration of the cells of tree and plant that the sap flows through and feeds the tree.

Even a stone is composed of tiny cells which breathe, just as the cells of your body, and just as your body as a whole does.

Every individual, be it cell, plant, animal or man, lives by vibrating; by expanding and contracting to take in the new and force out the old matter. Every mind, too, lives by vibrating—by alternately expanding to receive new ideas and contracting to get rid of the old.

Then there is another sort of vibration by which one individual communicates with another. Imagine to yourself that the ether is made up of infinitely small elastic balls. If you strike any one of those tiny balls it will strike those next to it and rebound, and those hit will strike the next, and so on the blow will travel from one tiny ball to the next, clear to the edge of creation—if you can imagine such a place. The blow you strike sets all the little elastic balls to vibrating, or moving back and forth.

Now if I stand away out in space and I feel the little elastic balls vibrate against me I know it means Something. By experience I learn what each kind of movement means.

If you clap your hands together the vibrations of those tiny elastic balls strike my ear and I say, "I hear some one clapping hands." If I face your way the vibrations strike my eyes and I say, "I see some one clapping hands." In any case your motion caused the ether to vibrate and I felt the vibrations.

If I had no ears or eyes I could not feel the vibrations, but they would be there just the same.

Every movement made sets the ether to vibrating to its particular pitch; and wherever there are eyes or ears the vibrations are recorded. When you talk it sets the ether going just the same whether there are ears to hear or not.

And when you keep perfectly quiet and think you set the ether going, too. Your brain sets vibrations going, just as your tongue does. There are people who can hear thoughts, just as you hear another's speech. In due time we shall all hear thoughts—we are all growing mental ears.

Thoughts are higher vibrations than spoken words; and they "carry" farther. You know a deep, growly bass voice makes a great noise when you are close to it, but a shrill treble call can be heard much farther than the growly bass. The high voice makes short, sharp, far-reaching vibrations.

Now thoughts make infinitely shorter, sharper and farther-reaching vibrations than the voice can; and thought vibrations carry farther and far more quickly. And wherever there is another thinker ready to hear, the thoughts are recorded.

Many times we hear the thoughts of other people and mistake them for our own; for everybody has at least a little mental hearing.

When you speak clearly and distinctly your voice carries much farther than if you speak hurriedly and carelessly; and other people can more readily understand what you say.

If you mumble your thoughts or your words the etheric vibrations carry mumbled meanings.

As people learn to think distinctly their thoughts carry farther and find more listeners. In course of time and with due practice, we shall easily think so that people on the other side of the earth can hear us. Not only that, but we shall think so clearly and high that the inhabitants of Mars and Venus and the sun, too, shall easily hear us.

I shouldn't wonder if what we call sun rays are really the thought vibrations of the sun's inhabitants. What if we receive and respond to their thoughts and think them our own!

Chapter XVII: The I Was and the I Am

According to the original Christian teaching (as I understand it), all undesirable conditions and circumstances are constituted by illusions that are held by ignorant, immature minds, and that project on to the bodily or material plane what may be compared to shadows. "If thine eye be single"—that is, if thy view be true, if thy understanding of life be sound,—"thy whole body shall be full of light. But if thine eye be evil, thy whole body shall be full of darkness." Undesirable experiences are the darkness wherein a person walks and works and stumbles about, whose notion of the universe, instead of shedding light on the meaning of life, casts on it a shadow. They are the effects produced on the field of our senses, by mistaken thought on the main issues of life, by a misunderstanding of life, by believing, and therefore practicing, a lie. The stuff they are woven of is something like the unsubstantial kind of stuff that makes up nightmares. They are the sort of thing from which Truth, thoroughly known, can set people free.

—J. Bruce Wallace.

Some one has said that "an honest man is the noblest work of God." Ten thousand thousand others have repeated his little speech—with a solemn wag of the head and sidewise squinting which conveyed the opinion that God is chary of his noble works.

Then there came another man who paraphrased that. "An honest God is the noblest work of man," he said. And a thousand or so of us wondered why we hadn't thought to say that! Why, of course. And the other thousands of thousands lifted up their hands and cried, "Blasphemy—stone him, stone him—put him out of the church, where the bogies'll get him!" They put him out. But the bogies haven't got him. And many of the thousands are taking up his cry—"An honest God is the noblest work of man."

Why not? An honest God is of greater value than many honest men, is he not? God is the creator of man; unless God is himself honest his honest man is but an accident, instead of an image and likeness of himself.

But, according to the paraphraser, man creates his God. Well, that is a paraphrase only, and true only in a sense.

God is. Man's creation of God is simply his mental concept of God; it is God as he sees him, or it, from his viewpoint.

An honest God is the concept of a man whose soul recognizes honesty and loves it. A God of power is the mental creation of him whose soul recognizes and loves power. A God of love is the mental creation of him who recognizes and loves love. A God of vengeance is the mental concept of him who loves vengeance.

Perhaps you think your mental concept of God is not so very important, since it is all in your mind and the real God is what he is regardless of your idea of him. But it matters vitally to you.

It is not God as he really is, that is creating you; but God as he appears to you. Your concept of God is creating you in its own image and likeness.

If you think of God as a great man on a throne, with a long white heard and an eye-for-an-eye-and-a-tooth-for-a-tooth expression, you may depend upon being made over into a sour-visaged decrepit old man who will want to die and get away from it all.

If you think of God as a God of power, love, wisdom, beneficence, you will aim to be perfect as he is perfect.

If you happen to be one of the fools who has said in his heart there is no God, your life will be a crazy patchwork and your end that of the stoic who defies earth to do its worst by him; which it probably will, being a willing earth and ready to give each according to his demands.

You are being created in the image and likeness of the Lord your God, the God enthroned in your heart.

What kind of a God is in your heart? Is he small and revengeful and capricious, a sort of policeman to tell your troubles to, to receive consolation from, and by whom to send punishment to your enemies?

Or is your God the Principle and Substance behind all creation, the power, wisdom, love, of all creation, a God who loves all, is just to all, generous to all, favors none?

But no matter how lofty a God you carry in your heart he will do you little good unless he is an "I Am" God.

Most men's Gods are "I Was" Gods. They believe God did wonderful things for the children of Israel; that he performed great miracles for the apostles and disciples of Jesus; but to this age they think of him as merely the I Was God, who stands aloof and lets man run things—man and the devil, or "malicious animal magnetism."

Believers in the "I Was" God are also great sticklers for the "I Shall Be" God, who is coming again to judge the wicked and set up his kingdom on earth. And these believers in the I Shall Be God think that their only business in life is to wait around until the great I Shall Be makes his appearance.

People who worship the "I Was" and the "I Shall Be" are never demonstrators. Between admiration of the "I Was" and anticipation of the "I Shall Be" they fall to the ground and—wait for the I Shall Be in themselves and others.

Only the "I Am" God does things. "I Am" love impels you to love now. "I Am" wisdom inspires you to act upon your ideas. "I Am" power performs miracles, not yesterday or tomorrow, but now.

I Am God is the God who works to-day, in you and in me. His ways are not the ways of the I Was God, nor of the I Shall Be God; they are the ways of the "I Am"—new, different, the ways of to-day, not of yesterday or to-morrow.

I know a dear woman who worships the I Was and the I Shall Be. She entertained Schlatter the healer, and was firmly convinced that he was a literal reincarnation of Jesus Christ. She took Schlatter's word for it. She also accepted his excuses for not immediately setting up a literal kingdom here on earth, as described in the book of Revelations. He told her he had other work to do just now, that he was going away, but would soon return and establish a literal kingdom. She swallowed it all—without a single chew. Schlatter went away, and later a body was found in the mountains which was said to be his.

Since Schlatter's disappearance some years ago, this lady has spent her time in writing about him and looking for his return. The I Was and the I Shall Be absorb her entire spiritual attention.

In the meantime she lives in a small mining town where in the life surging about her she sees no God. Not long ago she wrote me to help her speak the Word of freedom for a man on trial for his life. She said he was absolutely innocent and that a "terrible conspiracy" existed against him. The man was condemned to die, still protesting, not innocence but self-defense. It was a case of mix-up with two men and a woman, followed by a drunken brawl and the usual plea of "didn't mean to."

This lady's sympathies were all with the man, and her letters to me were pitiful. Her heart was wrung with agony for him and his bereaved wife, and convulsed with horror and impotent rage at the "wickedness" of the "wretches who falsely swore away his life." The way "evil" triumphed over justice was awful, she said, and she knew when Schlatter returned justice would be done and the wicked wretches annihilated—or words to that effect.

You see, she has no conception of an "I Am" God, who rules now. She sits in judgment on men's acts and prays to Schlatter to come back and set things right.

She remembers that the "I Was" put 10,000 to flight with Gideon's three hundred pitchers and candles—simply sneaked up and scared them into a panic. She knows the "I Was" hardened the heart of Pharaoh to lie repeatedly to the Israelites. She knows the devil had to ask permission of God before he tempted Job. She knows God said "I make peace and I create evil," and that "The Lord hath made all things himself; yea, even the wicked for the day of evil." She knows that "Whatsoever the Lord pleased that did he in heaven, and in earth, in the seas, and all the deep places." She knows all these things of the Great I Was.

But that the I Am works now in the hearts of men; that God now hardens one heart to perjury and another to truth, one to murder and another to lay down his life that his friend may live;—that God now works in these apparently antagonistic ways and thereby works out perfect justice, wisdom, love, has never entered her mind.

She cannot imagine that no man meets any form of death until he himself has ripened for that particular form of death. She has read that eighteenth chapter of Ezekiel, where God explains that every man dies for his own sins, not for the false swearings of another. But the great "I Was" said that, and the "I Shall Be" says it; but the "I Am" is absent—so she thinks.

Somewhere in the Old Testament—in Psalms, I think—the statement is made that those who die are "taken away from the evil to come." I opine that this is literally and unvaryingly true, that death never comes except as the dying one needed relief from worse things than death, things which lay straight ahead in his path.

The man of whom this friend wrote me deserved his death; if not for the specific act for which he was tried, then for other thoughts and acts which preceded that. The man was on the wrong road—a road of many and increasing evils. Death took him off the road at the right time, and gave him a better start in some other state of existence.

I must either believe this or deny the "I Am" God's power, wisdom or omnipresence. I must accept God's wisdom, power, love and presence on faith; or my own judgment on sight.

As I know from experience that appearances are deceitful, and that my personal judgment must perforce be based almost entirely upon appearances, I prefer to hold fast my faith in the presence, power, wisdom and love of the God over all. Therefore I deny that this man suffered an untimely death for the vindictiveness and perjury of others; I believe he died as a result of a mental constitution and tendencies which are hidden from me, but not from the I Am.

I believe it was the spirit of the I Am moving upon the face of his soul-deeps and saying, "Let there be light," which gave him his experiences and his particular form of death. And I believe his soul goes marching on to greater light—freed from the burdens of wrong habits of mind and body which were contracted in the old life of ignorance.

Oh, yes, it is easy to believe thus of one I never saw. It is not quite so easy to apply the same principle in the lives of those near and dear to me, and in my own life. But I aim to do it, even in the smallest details of living; and I am daily growing in the ability to acknowledge the "I Am" God in all my ways. I know this is the only way to live the new thought.

Chapter XVIII: Immortal Thought

The "I Am" of every being is God, the only power, wisdom, will, mind; the only actor in all action; the only creator, disintegrator and re-creator. The I Am of you is One, the Only One.

The "I Am" or ego or spiritual being of you is a thinker. All thinking is done by the one thinker—mortal thinking or immortal thinking.

Your body is an organization within you, the real you, the "I Am," the thinker,—an organization within you of the thoughts you (the I Am or God) are thinking. Your body is the present conclusion of all the thoughts, good, bad or indifferent, true or untrue, mortal or immortal, which you have thought, un-thought or rethought from the beginning of eternity; and hourly it is being changed by the new thoughts coming to you.

The real you does the thinking, recording conclusions in the body—which, mind you, is not you; nor does it even "contain" you; you are omnipresent, omnipotent, omniscient spirit or mind, and your body is within you. In you (God) it lives and moves and has its being, and by you (God) it is held together.

You have all-power to think all kinds of thoughts; and you use that power. You know you do—you know you think good thoughts, bad ones, mortal ones and immortal ones. Why question it?

You think all kinds of thoughts. But that does not make you all kinds of a being. You are the One Being to whom all kinds of thinking are possible, just as you are a being to whom all sorts of acts are possible.

In their essence, thought and action are one. Are you a human being when you play on the piano and an animal when you sweep the floor? Are you a human being when you walk and a fish when you go swimming? Of course not. You are the One Being whatever you choose to do or think—you are God-being.

One time you think mortal thoughts and the next time you think immortal thoughts (results always recording in your body) but always you are the same God-being.

And you feel all sorts of ways; but always you are you—the same One, God-being.

Your mortal thoughts are your thoughts of mortality—of death and all that leads to death—of sin, sickness, unhappiness, all that tends to discourage you from wanting to keep on living and thinking. Your immortal thoughts are your thoughts of life, activity, love, joy—all those thoughts which make you want to live more. One thought differs from another but you go on forever, the same One God-being.

Your mystification all comes from confounding yourself with your thoughts; from thinking of your thought-built body as you—which it is not.

In its deepest analysis your body and all your thoughts are purely mortal thoughts, and only your real you, the thinker, is immortal. To be immortal is to be subject to no change—which is true of Life Principle only. To be mortal is to be subject to change and death—which is true of all thought, even thoughts of life, love, joy.

All thoughts are fleeting and therefore "mortal" applies to them. Evil disappears before good thought, and "Good doth change to better, best."

The body is eternally changing—eternally receiving from the Self or spirit higher thought and eternally sloughing off lower thought. Body is mortal and will never be anything else. It will never cease to change; it will never cease to receive new thought and slough off back-number thought; it will never cease to "die daily." If it could for one hour cease this daily, hourly dying, this casting off thought which is out of date, it would die altogether.

Individual hanging on to dead thought is the cause of all old age and somatic death. The body instead of throwing off its dead and dying thought through its eliminative system, allows it to continue piling up in the body until death of the entire body comes as a relief. And the God-self goes on to new generations.

All bodily energy is the energy of live thought. Death comes to the body when dead thought preponderates. "Except ye become as a little child," whose daily dying is perfect, you shall continue to grow old and die the somatic death.

A child hangs on to nothing. Every new thing charms it completely from the old, and its intense mental and physical activities keep the old moving out and off to make room for more of the new.

Can you give any reason under the sun why human beings should not continue to live the child life and escape death of the body as a whole? There is no reason to be found in science, logic or nature; the one reason lies in our artificial living.

We stuff the mind with unused knowledge; we stuff the body with twice to ten times the food we need (all food is thought, too); we glory in "owning" more things than we can possibly need or use; we spend our time straddling our possessions to keep others from using them; is it any wonder we become literally loaded down until our bodies are too cumbersome for any life more strenuous than that of the grave?

Life to us is too real, too earnest; we want too much; and as long as we persist in living at this dying rate the grave will be our goal.

I said that in its last analysis all thought is mortal thought. This is true of formed thought, or thoughts.

Thought substance is eternal; thought substance is "matter," without beginning or end; and matter in its original state is mind or spirit—the One Thinker and his thought material, one and indivisible.

Thought substance is immortal, unchanging; but all forms of this thought substance are mortal, ever changing. Think of the ocean—the water is ever the same, but the waves, the forms assumed by the water, eternally change; so with thought substance and thought forms. The body being an organization of thought forms, of "mortal thoughts," must "die daily"; but that thought substance from which all its forms are made is immortal mind—is the God-self. Your body is simply a series or growing organization of fleeting eddies in your immortal God-self.

Too wonderful to grasp? Well, never mind—better not grasp it too tightly anyway—it might prove only another weight on your mind! Let the thought come and go in your consciousness, as waves come and go on the ocean; by and by you will "realize" that it is true— that you and the Father, body and soul, are all One and eternal. Just take it for granted, dearie, and love and be radiantly happy. So shall you use mortality to prove immortality.

Chapter XIX: God in Person

God [Universal Mind] is not a person; he is all persons.

"The Universe is One Stupendous Whole, Whose body Nature is, and God the Soul."

This means that "Nature," which includes man, is the body of God; and God's body is to him what your body is to you—a statement of beliefs which is eternally changing as experience teaches you more.

The only body God has is your body and mine; the only brains he has are your brains and mine; the only experience he has is your experience and mine; the only judgment he has is your judgment and mine.

The only way God has of proving anything is through your experience and mine.

You have heard it said that you cannot teach a man anything he does not already know; that to educate a man is to draw out into consciousness that which is already within him. By his own experience and by the teaching of others he becomes conscious of the wisdom which was all the time within him. All knowledge is latent in God (the Whole) just as it is in you; and God becomes conscious of what he knows by the same processes by which you become conscious. Your real self is God.

Watch yourself and you will see how God does things.

God is Wisdom. But Wisdom and knowledge are not identical. Knowledge is Wisdom proved—by the only proof, experience. All Wisdom is latent in God's soul, which is your soul and mine. God's Wisdom is expressed in his body, or "statement of beliefs," which is your body and mine.

God knows everything; but he knows that he knows only what he has proved through you and me, and all mankind and animal-kind and vegetable-kind.

"Some call it evolution; others call it God."

If God knew more he would not suffer through us. This is equivalent to saying if you and I knew more we would not suffer. There is no you and I; there is only God.

Evolution is simply God coming into consciousness of himself and his wisdom. Your body is a part of God's body; your soul is God, the One Life of all creation.

Do you wish to make his people suffer? Of course not. Do you wish to make yourself suffer? Of course you don't. You are God, and you don't intentionally make anybody suffer unless you think you have to. The rest of the suffering you have not yet learned to avoid. In other words, God has not yet learned how to avoid it.

But evolution still evolutes, and sighing and sorrow are already fleeing before the dawn of Wisdom coming to itself. God is learning how to enjoy himself in the flesh—in your flesh and mine.

What is flesh? It is mind. God is learning to enjoy himself in his own mind, which is your flesh and mine. He keeps on thinking through you and me until his "statements of belief," his flesh body, bring only joy to all creation and un-creation.

Why did he make the Ten Commandments? Why do you lay down laws unto yourself? Because you catch glimpses of higher things than you have yet experienced, and you lay down laws which you mean to live up to.

But you don't always live up to those laws, do you? Why? Because your body is an organization of intelligent cells each of which has a will of its own. You catch a glimpse of the truth that Love is the Greatest Thing in the World; you lay down a commandment: "Thou shalt not be impatient or angry." Before a day has passed you catch yourself breaking your commandment—"you forgot." In other words, the most intelligent cells in your body recognized a beautiful truth and promulgated a new commandment for all the cells to live by. But the less intelligent cells being still unconvinced of that beautiful truth, and being in a great majority, you did their will—you got mad.

Now God recognized through Moses most beautiful truths, and laid down laws to govern those who were as yet not intelligent enough to recognize the truths for themselves. For thousands of years God tried through these laws to make all the people see these truths. Thus his people evoluted—a little.

The God in Jesus caught a glimpse of still higher truth and laid down another law, that ye love one another. And still, after 2,000 years o that law, the people do not all see it, and very few of them obey.

A Moses or a Jesus recognizes truth so much greater than can be sensed by the common run of people, that it takes thousands of years of reiteration of that truth to make even a majority of the common run of people see it. It takes centuries of evolution really to convert the world to an Ideal conceived by a Jesus.

It takes you years of reiteration of your Ideal, and constant effort toward living up to it, before you can really convert your body to that Ideal.

In other words, God glimpses in Moses or Jesus a beautiful Ideal of himself; but it takes Him thousands and thousands of years to work out that Ideal, to evolute all people to the stage of wisdom and loving-kindness.

It is God's effort to work out his Ideals, which causes all suffering. This means that it is your effort to work out your Ideals, which causes all your suffering.

An Ideal impels change; the Established Order, in the Whole or a Part, resents and resists change; hence the pain. The spirit is willing but the flesh is established and refuses to change.

It was this Jesus had in mind when he said, "Resist not evil." The Established Order, the flesh, resists change because it is too shortsighted to see that the change is good. Because we are not yet convinced that All is Good and every change tends to greater good, we fight the change, more or less whole heartedly.

We have within us the same high Ideals, the same backslidings and wars, revolutions and evolutions, the same joys and sorrows, that the children of Israel had, that the universe at large has had and is having. All history is the history of your own thoughts. Man is an infinite little cosmos.

Just as in history ignorance has warred against the Ideal and yet in the fullness of time the Ideal has had its way; so in yourself ignorance wars against the Ideal and may for a time seem to win, but eventually the Ideal has its way. A man in his ignorance may yield to "temptation" but the results will take away the very temptation itself. When a child's fingers are well scorched it loses all desire to play with the fire.

There is no such thing as "ruining our lives forever." Every soul has all eternity in which to learn to live. Every soul is God—omnipresent, omniscient, or omnipotent in potentiality.

And all eternity is its school term, all space its school ground. Death is simply a promotion ceremony, peculiar to the kindergarten classes. A "ruined" life is no more than a "ruined" problem on Tommy's slate—it is wiped off to give Tommy, who has been learning by his mistakes, a chance to do a better sum.

Be still and know that God and you are one, and all things shall be made plain.

Chapter XX: How to Reach Heaven

The subjective or emotional self is the best of servants but the worst of masters.

All the evil in the world results from transposing authority from objective to subjective, from letting emotion run away with conscience and reason.

All unpleasant reactions are due to the waste of energy which results from this transposition of authority.

The emotional or subjective self is the storehouse of personal power; the objective self is the director of that power. Happy results come from intelligent use of power.

To give unbridled rein to the emotional self is like turning on the power of an automobile and then lying back and laughing—or weeping—whilst the auto runs its pace and kills or maims what comes in its way. The loud, hysterical giggle betrays that emotion is running away with the directing power, and that personal power is ebbing below the point of safety.

And the waste of power—the letting loose of more emotion than the occasion really calls for—is bound to produce its after effects of depression.

Depression of this sort is due to depletion of emotional energy, and disappears as the system recuperates—as more energy is stored.

Nearly all "blues" are caused by such reaction; energy is wasted in mental or physical agitation due to anger or fretting, or "righteous indignation," or excess of sympathy, or "having a good time"; and then we wonder why we are so blue. We go off and have a "good cry," which relaxes us, fall asleep after it, and wake up without the blues—and wonder why. More energy has been generated—that is all.

The secret of real enjoyment, of the kind from which there is no unpleasant reaction, lies in perfect control of the emotional nature; in so conserving your emotional power that it shall never be depleted beyond a certain definite point of poise, the point where there is plenty in well-controlled reserve.

When one first begins to find and maintain this state of poise he feels that he can never "have a good time" again—that he must repress all the fun and be glum and steady. But this is a mistaken idea, which will disappear as he gains control.

There are heights and depths and breadths of fun and joy which can never be touched except by the poised, controlled person. It takes emotional energy to enjoy, and the greater the store of energy the deeper the enjoyment, and the less of it is wasted in boisterous movements and noises.

One does not suppress his enjoyment of an incident; he suppresses unnecessary expressions of his enjoyment; and every such motion inhibited leaves him with that much more energy on hand with which to enjoy. In proportion as he ceases to slop his emotional power in loud laughs and unnecessary movements he deepens his power of enjoyment.

Laughs are on the surface; real enjoyment is in the deeps of being. It is the surface slopping one must suppress, the waste of power, that he may become conscious of the real depths of enjoyment.

Impulsiveness and nervousness are due to depleted emotional energy, and are invariably caused by letting the subjective, emotional self-rule. So much energy is wasted in unnecessary emotionalism that there is not enough left to enjoy with—there are no depths. There comes to be a habitual waste of emotion over the most trivial things, and there is no reserve for the greater things which occasionally come. All due to excessive expression of emotion. People who have not learned to control their expressions of emotion have never even tasted full enjoyment.

The one cure for nervousness, impulsiveness, boisterous emotionalism of all sorts is to be still; cut off all unnecessary waste and let the reservoirs fill.

There are two kinds of "lively dispositions." One is the result of hysterical slopping over of energy without regard to the fact that the reservoirs of personal power are dangerously near the point of utter depletion. This sort of liveliness often ends in tears, nearly always in depression.

The other sort of "lively disposition" is the surface expression of full reservoirs. One is like the slopping of water from a shallow bowl, by shaking the bowl; the other is like the rippling of a clear lake—the depths are clear, still and happy, whilst the surface answers brightly and without waste, to the passing breezes of fun. The bowl of water is exhausted by its expressions of fun; the clear lake enjoys its ripples of laughter without wasting itself.

The larger the lake the larger the waves. The same breeze which causes a pond to ripple will cause Lake Michigan to toss in white-capped glee. The greater the length, breadth and depth, the greater the waves; the greater the personal reservoir of emotional power; the bigger the laugh of which it is capable.

The loud laugh sometimes betrays the vacant mind and reservoirs; sometimes it betrays wide and deep and full ones; and by its ring the hearer can tell which. Who has not rippled in response to the musical, full, contagious loud laugh? And cringed at the sharp, hysterical loud laugh?

The musical laugh loud or soft, invariably indicates well stored reservoirs of emotional power and real enjoyment. The shrill unmusical laugh, the nervous laugh, loud or soft, invariably means nervous or emotional depletion, shallow reservoirs, and shallow enjoyment or none at all.

Musical and unmusical speaking voices are other indications of these states of personal power. Smooth, graceful, intelligent gesticulations are yet other indications of full reservoirs; rough, jerky unnecessary motions indicating depletion.

The curtailing of wasteful laughs and motions is one of the most important things in life. Emotion is soul force, that which accomplishes all the great things of life as well as all the little things.

Every human being has access to unlimited soul force, which is constantly flowing into him from the Universal Reservoir. But if he uses it as fast as it flows in—uses it in overdoing the small and least necessary things of life,—he has no power for the greater things every soul longs to do.

How much power would the world get from the Niagara River if it were not for the great natural dam and reserve power at the falls? If you would do the great things you must see that your energy is not wasted in a steady stream of little things.

Every movement, every thought, uses a definite amount of emotional energy. Every inhibition of a movement or thought stream permits the higher rising of your reservoir; just as every stone added to a dam increases the reservoir and power behind it.

There are enough good things to do and think in this beautiful world without dissipating our power in thoughtless activities, such as tapping our feet or fingers, rocking to and fro, giggling shrilly, and so on. Yes, we learn to do things by doing them; but do we want to do these useless things? Of course not. They are wasteful, unbeautiful.

And we can learn to stop them by stopping them; and have so much deeper power with which to do the useful, beautiful things. A half hour a day used in simply being still, will add almost incredibly to the depth of our reservoirs. And every time we remember to inhibit an unnecessary rock or tap or fidget we add another depth to our power. This is all easily proved by a little practice.

Our energy is soul power, which is also wisdom. As our energy deepens our wisdom deepens also, and our sense of humor deepens. Soul power is love and wisdom, the One and Only Substance of which the individual is an inlet—a small or large inlet according as he lets the energy run out fast, or conserves it for large uses; according as he lets it run, or dams it for personal use.

There is plenty of soul power for everything—yes. But it takes time to build a dam; and the man who lets loose his whole Niagara Falls of emotion upon trivial occasions will have to spend most of his time in patching his dam. And the man who dribbles all his power in thoughtless and useless acts has no power behind his Niagara.

Do you see that self-control is the key of heaven? And the time to use it is now, the place here.

"Earth's crammed with heaven" waiting to be conserved to individual uses. Love, power, wisdom is flowing through you into expression—don't let it flow too fast—don't waste it in thoughtless, foolish expression.

Cut off the wastes; use the power in wise directions, and let the tide rise within you. Thus shall you come to the great things you would do, and behold within you shall be the power to do them with joy; and there shall be no aftermath of depression.

This is heaven—the highest heaven for the deepest soul. And the door is open for everybody.

Vital energy is soul energy—love-power and wisdom mixed—L2W2.

The body is a generator of vital or soul energy.

Heaven and hell are states of bodily being. The body full of vital or soul energy—L2W2—experiences heaven.

The body depleted of its soul energy lives in hell—-carried there by riotous living, by wasting its vital or soul energy.

Chapter XXI: A Look at Heredity

No evolutionist can overlook heredity, nor underestimate it. He believes that every generation comes in on the shoulders of its predecessors, and he fully appreciates the value of good predecessors The world's pride of ancestry is not so foolish as it might appear.

The more intelligence and culture my forbears had the greater my possibilities. There are no breaks in the law of growth or evolution or heredity, though the casual observer often fancies there are.

Every human being comes into the world as an "acme of things accomplished" by his ancestors, and he is an "encloser of things to be" accomplished by himself and his descendants.

But who are my ancestors? Let me tell you that Ralph Waldo Emerson and Jesus of Nazareth are more directly my ancestors than many of those whom the world calls my great-grandfathers. There is a spiritual and mental kinship through which we inherit.

There are spiritual and mental relationships to which we all owe far more of our goodness and greatness than can be traced to those of blood tie. In rare instances only do these spiritual and mental relationships exist within the line of blood relationship.

The world does well to be proud of its ancestry; but it does better when it appreciates its spiritual ancestry. Think you that the poor little waif owes a larger inheritance to the woman who bore it and deserted it, than to the foster parents who nurtured it in love and wisdom?

Our blood relations are not the only relations from whom we inherit; neither when we are born do we cease to inherit. There is One Father of us all, and the oft-repeated statement that we are all brothers and sisters is no fanciful one. The "fatherhood of God and brotherhood of man" is fact; and the man who thinks he is limited by the ignorance of his blood relations is himself an ignoramus. If his blood relations are not to his liking, let him draw a new inheritance from the world's greatest and best. They, too, are his ancestors.

And mark this: Not only does the son inherit from his fathers of blood or spirit tie, but many a father inherits from the son that which the son has gained from other sources than those of blood relationship.

Inheritance by blood tie is not a stream, the outlet of which can rise no higher than its source. Rather, it is a sort of hydraulic ram through which life may be coaxed to almost any height of culture and refinement.

I have heard it said that culture is "the soul of knowledge—the essence of right living" inherited from our ancestors. Where did they get it? I will tell you where; they got it by persistence in the same sort of practices which are decried—by "wresting, by force," the knowledge, wealth and dominion of others; by generations of "monastic seclusion," much of it enforced by others whose turn it was to "wrest by force"; by generations of "rigid self-control"; by hours and days and years of prayer, which is simply a phase of "going into the silence"; and, yes, and even by "breathing like a filthy, crazy Yoga"—though much of the breathing was forced by strenuous endeavors to get away from the raging hordes whose wealth or daughters they were stealing. The Spirit of Evolution which is running this universe is very cunning in devices for inducing self-culture.

Full breathing, going into the silence, affirmations, etc., are not new methods of self-culture. They are as old and their practice as universal as life itself. But heretofore their practice has been in the main compulsory. Humanity had to be persecuted, starved, hunted into breathing, exercising, praying—had to be forced to develop body, soul and wits by using them.

The present generation inherits the wisdom gained through their efforts. Not the least of its inheritance lies in its wits developed to the point of seeing that for self-development, ten minutes of voluntary deep breathing is preferable to an all-day chase to save one's neck; that a half hour of intelligent silence is worth more than the three and four hour "wrestlings with the Lord" such as our great-grandfather John Wesley—and many of his inheritors—practiced regularly.

Herein lies the great difference between our ancestors and us. They were by conditions compelled to self-culture; whilst we, their inheritors, are making intelligent use of it.

Through evolution we are learning to conserve energy. Our ancestors spent all their time—perforce—in half-unconscious physical exercise and breathings; we spend a few minutes a day in intelligent exercise and breathing, and conserve our forces for mental and spiritual uses.

And without them [our ancestors] we should be minus the intelligence to do this. Humanity is a solidarity—on the square; and without the work of his ancestors none shall be made perfect.

But it is by the work of his ancestors that man stands on to-day's pinnacle. What they learned to do by labored effort and mainly under compulsion, we do by instinct.

It is by man's work to-day on this pinnacle, that his great-grandchildren shall be brought forth on yet higher pinnacles, with yet higher instinctive knowledge.

Take the most cultured person you know; trace his ancestry and tell me where his culture began. You cannot do it. Go clear back to William the Conqueror if you will; thus far you may call his ancestors cultured, but even so their culture, all the way back, is a descending scale of boorishness in comparison with what we twentieth century folk call culture. And we must hark back of William for the beginning of his culture.

William the Conqueror was the illegitimate son of Robert the Devil. Did culture begin with Robert? And the mother of William was a miller's daughter. Is she the mother of all culture?

Robert the Devil was the third earl of Normandy; which means that his grandfather was an ordinary everyday scrub who probably murdered somebody particularly obnoxious to the king and was rewarded with an earldom. Did he bequeath "the soul of knowledge, the essence of right living," to William the Conqueror and his exclusive progeny? If so, where did he get it?

His own grandfather and the ancestors of the poor miller's daughter roamed the same woods, fought the same battles, hunted the same beasts and men, and gnawed the same bones. Where did the ancestors of Robert the Devil pick up the "soul of knowledge"? And what were the miller's ancestors doing whilst Robert's grandfathers cornered the "essence of right living"? For I warrant you that William's miller's-daughter-mother was less of a stranger to the "soul of knowledge, the essence of right living" than was that devil of a Robert.

Yes, there are many people who are educated but not cultured. But their progeny will brag of their culture. For what is in one generation mere education, or "monastic seclusion," or "rigid self-control," or "going into the silence," or "breathing like a filthy, crazy Yoga," is by time and unconscious cerebration transmuted into pure "culture."

And if any of us lack culture you may depend upon it our ancestors, by blood and spirit, are numbered among those who failed to "wrest by force" the very things decried as uncultured.

All life is education; and time transmutes education into culture, "the soul of knowledge, the essence of right living."

Not a human effort but is necessary to the development of the soul of knowledge. Not a Yoga breath, not an hour of silence, not a moment of rigid self-control, not a day of hard labor, not a sound or movement or cry of joy or sorrow or rage or despair,—not one but has helped to free the soul of knowledge. Not one could have been dispensed with without leaving culture less cultured than it is.

The difference between education and culture is the difference between the daily drill at the piano and the finished musical expression of a Paderewski.

Education comes first and without it there can be no culture. Education is the work of *today*; whilst culture is the soul of well used yesterdays. Why exalt the well used yesterdays to the disparagement of today's opportunities?

Inheritance is wealth left us by sanguine and spiritual relations gone before. It is capital left us, to be increased by just such "wresting by force" as some people condemn. Who is the more valuable to the human race:—he who parades his inheritance as he received it or he who adds to it his own efforts at self-culture?

Don't get stuck on tradition and kowtow eternally to heredity. Be an Individual and improve heredity. If your inheritance was poor make it better; if it was good make it better. The world's culture is only just beginning; get busy helping it along. That is the important thing.

Do it now.

Chapter XXII: Critic and Criticized

"I don't want to be criticized."

"But you want to learn, don't you? You surely are not satisfied that you know it all."

"Oh, of course I want to learn, but I want to learn by myself. I would rather be wrong than be criticized. I hate to be told how to do things. I want to find out for myself."

Solomon the Wise reasons not thus. Solomon prayed for wisdom above all things, and in receiving wisdom he received all else.

The man who thinks he would rather be wrong than be criticized is for the time being a moral coward and no Solomon. He values his "feelings" of the moment above wisdom. He does not want wisdom and knowledge above all things; he wants what wisdom and knowledge he can gain without the sacrifice of his feeling of self-complacency.

He is complacent as long as his friend says to him, "You are a good fellow, a very admirable fellow"; he feels good as long as he thinks his friend considers him wise; he expands and smiles, and works away in his own good way.

In his moments of confidence he will tell his friend that Wisdom and Knowledge are the greatest things in the universe; that we grow only by the acquisition of Wisdom and Knowledge; that growth is Life, and Life is Love or God. He will enthuse a bit and tell you Wisdom is God, the One Desirable One; and that by growing in wisdom man becomes conscious of his divinity.

Just here his friend, who is a prosy, practical sort of fellow, interrupts him. "See here, Smith," he says, "you are not running this branch of your business quite right. You just ought to see how Thomson does that sort of thing."

He gets no farther; Smith freezes instantly, and Jones's confidences catch the vibrations. Smith is "so sensitive, you know"—he would rather not know anything about better methods, than to stand the shock of a criticism. Jones talks about the weather a bit, and departs.

Smith continues to think he desires wisdom above all things. He doesn't. He desires above all things to have his bump of approbativeness smoothed.

He fails to know himself. And he will not learn himself, because he refuses all truth which does not make him "feel" good.

He shuts himself off from a thousand avenues by which wisdom is trying to reach him.

It is said our enemies are our best friends. Emerson bids us listen to them and learn of them.

Burns exclaims:—

"O wand some power the gift give us
To see ourselves as others see us!
O wand from money a blunder free us
And foolish notion."

Our critics are answering Love's attraction to free us from blunders and foolish notions.

Why not? Why resent a criticism? We are all members of "One Stupendous Whole." Why resent and refuse another's suggestion? It is our own suggestion, drawn by our own affirmed love for wisdom and knowledge.

We don't understand ourselves; we don't trust our surroundings. We say we want wisdom above all things; we want to understand. In our heart of hearts we do love wisdom above all things; therefore we attract it through all avenues.

It is our soul's love for wisdom and knowledge which attracts to us the criticisms of friend and foe.

If we really believed that we attract what we receive; that "our own" comes to us; that all things are working together to gratify our soul's desires;—if we really believed all this we would meet criticism in a friendly spirit, with senses alert to find the kernel of wisdom it is bringing us.

To resent a criticism is to re-send, to send away, a bit of knowledge your soul has been praying for. All because your bump of approbativeness has an abnormal appetite for prophecies of "smooth things."

But to re-send a criticism is not to get rid of it. It comes back to you over and over, and perhaps every time in a little ruder form.

If you speak softly to a friend and he fails to hear, you repeat in a louder tone; if he is very deaf you holler, and perhaps touch his shoulder to gain his attention.

All creation is alive, and pursues the same tactics. When you resent (re-send) a criticism, Creation sends it back at you a little more emphatically. If you still resent it Creation puts still more force into repeated sendings. She keeps this up, in answer to your own semi-conscious desire for wisdom and knowledge, until by some hook or crook you take the kernel of knowledge contained in that criticism. Then Creation smiles and lets you alone—on that line.

The way to avoid Creation's kicks is to accept her hints as they come to you in the form of friendly criticism or suggestion.

Not all criticisms are true in their entirety, but every one contains somewhere a suggestion by which you may profit—by which you may grow in wisdom and knowledge.

Don't let that one little bump of approbativeness make you re-send that knowledge—and bring down Creation's kicks to drive it home.

But don't get the idea that that little round nub of approbation is "bad." He is not. He is a good and useful member of your family, and deserves to be well fed and cared for and respected.

But feed him so well on your own good opinions that he will not sulk and kick if he doesn't receive unlimited taffy from others. Get away up high in your own opinion. Know yourself a god, unique, indispensable to Creation. You have powers and wisdom and knowledge not possessed by anybody else in the world. Nobody who ever lived or ever will is any better or any more of a god than you are.

Neither is anybody less good or less of a god than you. We are different—that is all. Every man has his individual goodnesses and his peculiar point of view—no better than yours, but different.

It takes every man in the world to see all sides of anything, or anybody.

Every individual who is at all wise wants to see all sides of things. The only chance he has of doing this is to look at things from other people's points of view, as well as his own; to put himself in other people's places; to see as others see; to vibrate with the other fellow—who sees another side of the same thing.

Listen to your critic. See yourself as he sees you. He is your best friend, drawn in answer to your soul's cry for more wisdom and knowledge. Be friends with him. Hush the clamor of approbativeness with your own high affirmations of your goodness and worth—hush the clamor and listen. The spirit in you will separate the chaff from the wheat of the criticism; a smiling little "Poof!" will blow away the chaff; and your soul will expand and increase in stature by assimilating the wheat.

Chapter XXIII: The Nobility

We always come in contact with the people we live and think up to. If you are not satisfied with the present environment it can be changed by making your very best of it, and in the meantime fitting yourself mentally, physically and in deportment, for the sort of people you want. Get ready for 'em.

And see you waste no energy in impatience over having to wait a long time.

It takes mental and physical culture and gracious deportment to fit you for the sort of friends you want.

There is no place in life which does not offer plenty of advantages for the cultivation of all these things, but especially for the cultivation of a gracious deportment. You may depend that if you can be lovely and gracious to "common people," who may ruffle your feathers the wrong way, you will be at home if a duchess happens along.

Duchesses, you know, belong to the class of people who make a study and lifelong practice of being lovely and gracious. I am talking about real duchesses now—not the kind that get rich quick and marry a title without having the real qualifications of nobility.

Somebody has said that the world is divided into two classes, the civil and the uncivil. The hall-mark of real nobility is the habit of being civil to the uncivil. No better place to acquire this gentle art than living among the uncivil.

The youth who finds himself among the uncivil and who proceeds to cultivate uppishness and contempt for his associates; who "looks down" on those with whom he is compelled to associate; who tries to be "superior" and to impress others with his superiority,—such an one is forever fixing himself in the class of the uncivil—where duchesses don't grow.

You are what you are. Time spent in trying to "impress" people is worse than wasted. Be your gracious self, and honor not only your father and your mother but your next door neighbor and your next door neighbor's kitchen maid if you want to develop the qualities that will fit you for the sort of associates you want—members of the really truly nobility.

Cultivate your brains, dearie; cultivate your body; cultivate your soul; all to the best of your ability. But above all and in all and through all cultivate the mental and physical deportment of the truly noble. Belong always to the civil class and practice civility eternally upon the uncivil as well as upon the civil.

When a brawling enemy followed Pericles home one dark night, with intent to injure him, Pericles sent his own servant with a lantern to light the man home again. Pericles did not descend from his own class to pay his uncivil enemy in his own coin.

Go thou and cultivate Pericles and thine own high self. Then shall all desirable associates seek you, instead of you having to seek them.

Greater credit belongs to him who sees the real nobility through the housemaid's dress and manner, than to him who recognizes it in silk and velvet voice.

We are all members of the nobility, all descended through Adam and Eve, who never saw silk nor made salaams. All are sons and daughters of the Most High.

Don't be fooled into contempt and incivility by our masquerade costumes; and don't value some of our gowns above ourselves—or yourself.

L' Envoi.
When earth's last picture is painted,
    And the tubes are twisted and dried,
When the oldest colors have faded,
    And the youngest critic has died, We shall rest—and, faith, we shall need it—
    Lie down for an aeon or two,
Till the Master of All Good Workmen
    Shall set us to work anew.
And those that were good shall be happy—
    They shall sit in a golden chair;
They shall splash at a ten-league canvas
    With brushes of comet's hair.
They shall find real saints to draw from—
    Magdalene, Peter, and Paul; They shall work for an age at a sitting,
    And never get tired at all.
 And only the Master shall praise us,
    And only the Master shall blame;
And no one shall work for money,
    And no one shall work for fame;
But each for the joy of the working,
    And each in his separate star,
Shall draw the thing as he sees it,
    For the God of things as they are.

Just How To Wake The Solar Plexus

Table of Contents:

Chapter I: I Am The Sun Of God

Do you desire above all things to live a serene, useful, successful life? Do you want to get out of the petty limitations of conventionality? Out of pain and sin and sickness? Away from the small hurts of every-day living? Do you really want to get away from them? Are you willing to work out the salvation that is in you?

Or would you rather sit still and grumble at the universe in general and everybody in particular? Do you desire health and prosperity, happiness and a wider usefulness enough to work every day and all day for them, as a man works who desires to be a great musician, or artist, or scholar? Or do you just weakly wish that somebody would carry you bodily "on flower beds of ease" to a heaven of happiness and prosperity? Are you *resolved* to have health, happiness and material prosperity, and to be more widely useful, no matter what it costs nor how long it takes?

Then you will have them. You will, without the shadow of a doubt, get there. You could not fail if you tried. And I *am* with you all the way and at the same time I *am* already there, and I will tell you something that was an immense help to me in getting there. It was the sun. Shelton says the sun is God. I should not be surprised if he is right. But I am not sure he is.

However, the sun helped me to a realization of my Self, my all-wise, all-loving, all-powerful, serenely happy Self. Your self is just as grand as my self, and you are dead certain to find your self, when once you set about it.

The reason you have not already found it is that you have put in most of your time in watching the self of other people. You have been impolite to your Self. You have consulted every Tom, Dick and Harry before your Self. And you have called your Self all sorts of names. No wonder he has crawled into his shell and pulled the hole in after him! No wonder you think he doesn't know much!

But he does, and he will do anything for you if you just be even half way civil to him! Be polite and respectful to your Self. Tell him he is a pretty good fellow after all – the best friend you have. Ask his advice, and use it. And let him do things for you. All he wants is *recognition*, and he will do anything you want done, and do it better than anybody else can do it for you.

The sun helped me to make a close acquaintance with my Self. He will also help you. Did you ever think how much alike are Son and Sun? Jesus was the Son of God. I studied the life of that Son for years, trying to be like Him. My success was indifferent.

But one day it suddenly flashed across my mind that *I am the Sun* of God! That was to me a glorious idea that took possession of me and literally transformed me by the renewing of my mind.

That is a little trick ideas have – give them a lodging and they will make a whole new house for you, a "house not made with hands."

"*I am the Sun* of God" made me all over in no time.

I will tell you some of the changes it made in me: I used to be very "sensitive"; so much so that I didn't know my own mind more than half the time; and I was always getting my feelings hurt; though I was generally too proud to show it.

I tried desperately to conquer my feelings and keep from being hurt, but success did not crown my efforts nor even perch upon my banner.

At last I grew tired of coddling my feelings and I told them, with considerable righteous indignation, to keep on feeling hurt till they got tired and quit – they would receive no more attention from me! They did get tired and quit. The sun warmed up my feelings and happified them for good and all.

This is the way of it: I said to myself, "If *I am the Sun* of Good, then my one reason for being is simply to radiate – to shine – to send out good thought."

Now, you see, that is just where I had been making a vital mistake. I had always tried to be a Moon instead of a Sun. The Moon is cold, dark, sterile, receptive, only shedding reflected light. I had been all the time receiving everything – other people's ideas and opinions, and even all kinds of hurts from them! And, as if this was not enough receiving, I daily besought God to give, give, *give* me the Holy Ghost, not to mention the hundred and one other favors I begged! – of Him and other folks.

And all this time I was really a *Sun*, the Sun of God, made for the one purpose of sending out, instead of receiving. I had "life in myself," as "the Father hath life in Himself."

In order to outgrow entirely all that sensitiveness I had simply to remember, when my feelings were injured, that I *am* a Sun made to shine, instead of a Moon made to receive hurts from without.

Every human being is literally a Sun of Good, made to radiate. If he will attend strictly to the business of sending out Good Will, as the sun radiates beams, he will soon find his feelings under his control.

Suppose every time somebody on this planet grumbled at Old Sol, he were to curl up within himself and fail to send forth his rays. If he were "sensitive" like most people that is what he would do. But Sol is too wise a god for that. He attends strictly to his own business of shining. So positively does he shine, and so fully is he absorbed in doing his best, that he shines upon not only the "just," who appreciate his shine, but he shines joyously on the "unjust," who only grumble in return. So positive is that blesses old Sol that he never feels a grumble! His shine just meets the grumble and transmutes it before it touches him.

The reason we get hurt by the unkind words of those about us is that we forget to shine.

The Sun Within

There is a real sun center in us, the Solar (or Sun) Plexus. This is a great nerve center situated in back of the stomach. When this central Sun, from which all the nerves of the body radiate, is in its normal condition, it steadily radiates a real energy, just as the sun does. This energy vibrates through the nerve highways and by-ways of the body out toward the surface of the body in all directions (the mucous membranous surface, as well as the outer skin), and is thrown off in a real halo or atmosphere, which always envelops the body. If this radiation from the Solar Plexus is positive enough, the influence of another person cannot disturb its steady, harmonious vibrations in the least.

And a person who is thus positively radiant wields an immense power for good to those less positive than himself. His presence alone, without a spoken word or even a definitely directed thought, stills the troubled minds with which he comes in contact.

In all human beings, who have not yet learned the law of being, the Solar Plexus is in a cramped condition that prevents the steady flow of life, or "nerve ether," to all parts of the body. From this cause comes every disease of the human race – mental, physical or environmental.

All one's "feelings" are due to the action or inaction of this Sun-center. Good feelings are due to free action; ill feelings to contraction. Pleasant sensations are caused by the outflow of "nerve ether," energy, Life; unpleasant sensations by an interruption of the steady outflow.

In every human being there is a steady radiation of Life, or Love, or Good Will from the Solar Plexus, except when the individual himself interrupts the radiation when he contracts the Solar Plexus, thus diminishing the outflow, or interrupting it altogether as in death.

A continued contraction of the nerves results in a chronic state of nervous collapse. The nerves literally collapse, as does a soft tube from which fluid is withdrawn.

The nerves are tubes for the conveyance of Life to all parts of the body. Contract the Solar Plexus and you withdraw Life from the body.

The Solar Plexus is the point where life is born – where the Uncreate becomes Create; the unorganized becomes organized; the unconscious becomes conscious; the invisible appears; that which is dimensionless becomes measurable.

There is positively no limit to the amount of life this solar center in the individual is able to generate, and no limit to the rapidity with which it may be generated.

But this omnipotent sun-center is a generator of blind energy, all-mighty but unintelligent in any high sense.

The Solar Plexus is a *servant* to the brain. No more life is generated (i.e., made visible) than the brain of "God in the highest" dictates. Every minute contraction and expansion of the sun-center of Life is in obedience to the brain. No lightest fancy of the brain but is responded to instantaneously by the Solar Plexus.

Do you perceive why and how it is that "of every idle word shall ye give account?" And how ye shall be "rewarded according to the deeds done in the flesh?"

What you sow in imagination you will surely reap in the body. What you have sown in thought you are reaping now.

Conscious thought is master of the sun-center, from which flows the life of your body; and the quality of your body, including the brain, determines the quality of your environment. You are your own lord and master, the arbiter of your own destiny.

Now do you see why a "sensitive" person gets "hurt" continually? He thinks he is a Moon instead of a Sun; he receives from others words or tones or acts which displease him; he contracts the sun-center of himself, stopping his radiation of Good Will.

"It is the stoppage of his own radiations of life or good will that hurts him, *not* the thing that was said or done. And he alone is the Lord of that Sun-radiator; therefore he hurts himself. I made this discovery by actual experience, and have demonstrated the fact that nobody on earth has the power to "hurt my feelings." By studying the action of the real sun and remembering that I *am the Sun of God*, I quickly learned the art and acquired the habit of shining. "What I do ye may do also."

Chapter II: "The Lord Our God Is A Consuming Fire"

Did you ever notice that the sun makes no special effort to destroy that which is not fit to live? The same steady shine which gives life to the growing plant causes fermentation, death and transmutation to everything which is cut off from the source of its life.

As soon as I learned that I am the Sun of God I knew that I need make no special effort to destroy "evil" – the "carnal mind." I saw that I had simply to shine, like Old Sol, and the radiation from me would transmute mind and body and environment for me.

That conception afforded me infinite relief. I saw that all the good I had been so assiduously endeavoring to force into myself was already mine if I would only "let my light shine" to ripen it.

I discovered also that to let my light shine is a matter of choice, not feeling, so I chose to let the light shine out from my solar center and I abandoned myself to that radiation. No more worry for me over "evil" thoughts or acts. I just let the Sun shine upon them.

I discovered that Jesus of Nazareth had a level head – "I say unto you that ye resist not evil," is the very acme of wisdom.

I had pondered often and long upon that injunction of His, without being able to see the philosophy of it, and I simply could not obey it.

Why? Because *I am good* and must, from the compulsion of my own law of being, be forever "set over against" evil. If I know no better way of getting rid of evil than to fight it, then fight I must. But the more I fight the greater the evil will grow.

At last in sheer despair, I may be still and think; when I shall see that non-resistance will conquer where resistance worse than fails.

Do you see yet why this is so? The Solar Plexus is the radiating center of life, the center from which flows the divine energy, love, that can overcome (cause to "come over") all evil. We can overcome evil with good; we can love our enemies into friends; we can "overcome' them; i.e., cause them to "come over."

Please remember that love is not sentimental gush; it is not a matter of words; but it is a steady radiation of good will from the solar center, and may or may not be expressed in word or deed. But it will be expressed in either word or deed as the need of the "enemy" calls it forth. But whether expressed or not, that steady, silent radiation of Good Will, or Love, will transmute enemies into friends, "evil" into good, just as certainly as the sun rays will make pure that which was impure.

This being true, the one thing necessary is to let the solar center radiate Good Will all the time.

Until we understand and take control of ourselves, every thought that passes through the mind affects the action of the Solar Plexus. Thoughts that are pleasant to us cause the center to open and radiate Good Will or Love. Every unpleasant thought causes it to contract, thus shutting off the supply of good will, love, life, from the body, brain and environment.

Non-resistant thought expands the Solar Plexus; resistant thought contracts it. Now do you see what a good scientist Jesus was?

"And I say unto you that ye resist not evil." If a man would have you go a mile with him, go two miles willingly; let your Good Will radiate; and by the time you have finished your second mile his Solar Plexus will be vibrating with yours, and you will both be the wiser and more loving for your journey.

But that will depend upon how you take his invitation or command. You can go under protest, asserting your own righteousness and his injustice; in which event he will conquer you, and you will have obeyed the letter, but not the spirit of Jesus' injunction.

Or you may envelop yourself with the air of a martyr – which is mighty thin covering, by the way – and go with him because it's your "duty" to do a lot of unpleasant things you would much rather leave undone. This is the air lots of women assume with their husbands and children – the injured air. They go a mile – oh, yes, two miles, or three – with their brows uplifted and their lips pursed up with "prunes and prisms," and a very loud humility of manner. All of which brings the inconsiderate husband or children to time – for a time. They feel that they have committed the unpardonable sin, and hasten to humble themselves and make amends. But by and by they become hardened – and the last state is worse than the first. You see it is not so much the thing you do as the way you do it.

I said, before we understand and take command of ourselves, every thought passing through the mind either expands or contracts the solar center of being. We must learn to control the action of the Solar Plexus just as we learn to control the action of the fingers in learning to play the piano; by thought and careful exercise.

Anybody can play the piano who will, and anybody can learn self-control who really wants to. And when he really wants to he will. Until that time you might just as well let him alone. As long as a man prefers to let his Solar Plexus flop around like a weathercock on a squally day, registering all the silly, thoughtless or malicious things his neighbor may say, why just let him flop. He will get tired of such buffetings by and by, and begin to control himself and his "feelings." Nobody can do it for him.

"Practice makes perfect." He who puts in the most time in faith-full practice will accomplish most in the shortest time. The man who puts in an hour a day in practicing "concentration" exercises and then lives the remainder of his time on the old plane of resentment and resistance, will not make half the progress of the man who spends little or no time in "exercises," but endeavors to put his good will into each act and thought of the day, every day in the week.

Every experience, little or big, is an "exercise" for developing concentration. You no more need special hours for the development than a cat needs two tails. Put your mind and good will into what you are doing, and re-put it every time you catch it flying the track.

Make up your mind to keep your light shining, your solar center expanded, no matter what happens or how you feel." Of course you can't do it at first, any more than you can play the piano by simply "making up your mind" to do it. Your hands will get out of position and your fingers will persist in being thumbs; but, nevertheless, if your mind is made up, you will keep at it until you teach your hands to keep their correct positions and your fingers to touch the keys daintily and truly, with scarcely a conscious thought.

Just so with the Solar Plexus; by practice you can teach your solar center to radiate Good Will, no matter what is happening outside of you or within, or how much your thought may be occupied with other things.

That is heaven, where I am. And the door is wide open – with "welcome" written above.

Let your light so shine that men may see your good works: — your love-sun-shines – and glorify your *I am God* which is heaven.

Chapter III: Just Why And Just How

The Solar Plexus, or sun center, is to the human body precisely what the visible sun is to the solar system. It is the source of all life and light; it is the manufacturer of life and light.

The sun manufactures light and heat by inhaling that which transcends light and heat. The sun breathes. It inhales "spirit" and exhales light and heat – intelligent will.

The Solar Plexus inhales light and heat and exhales magnetism; another form of intelligent will; a finer form; a more intelligent will, and therefore more powerful as well as finer.

If the sun were to cease breathing, there would be nothing left for the Solar Plexus to breathe. Life would cease to manifest. If the sun were to breathe spasmodically, only half filling itself with "spirit," then would there be a poverty of light and heat. The effect of such a poverty of light and heat you can see in plants or persons kept in dungeons.

We are wont to believe that man breathes with his lungs alone, when the truth is that he breathes with every cell of his body. And each pore of his body, inside and out, is an avenue for the transmission of sunlight and heat to the great laboratory of the body, the Solar Plexus. The Solar Plexus is the body's breathing center, where sunlight and heat are transmuted to magnetism.

All disorders of the human body and brain are due to shutting off the sun's rays before they can reach the Solar Plexus. The deep and regular breather *cannot* be sick or mentally weak.

Just one thing prevents the breath from reaching the solar center; a closing of the pores, outward and inward. A stooping position will cramp and close many of the lung pores; tight clothing will shut up not only lung pores, but others as well. But first and last and always, and with more power than is contained in all other things combined, will *the Mind* contract the pores and rob body and brain of life and light.

Fear is the great robber. Watch the effect of a single fear upon yourself — see how you cringe, shrivel and contract; see how you clinch your hands and curl up your toes; see how you expel the air from your lungs and hold it expelled; and you can guess, at least, how fear keeps you out of your own. This cringing and curling and shrinking is habit with the human race. Human beings are trained to fear past, present and future; themselves and their "enemies," not to mention their friends; trained to fear what is without and what is within; fear the devil and God, too. Is it any wonder fear is a habit, and a good, full breath an unheard of thing to the majority of human beings? The one problem of the human race is to get rid of the fears so assiduously cultivated for so many ages. No need to tell the fearless one to "breathe freely." He does it without thought of effort. As a consequence, his body is large and strong.

Every effort of the individual is for the one purpose of freeing him to breathe; to inhale intelligent will; retain it until it has rejuvenated every cell and become tinctured with the essence of his being; and to *exhale* it as still more intelligent will for the accomplishment of his purposes. Man breathes in intelligent will; focuses it within; and radiates it in new and more powerful form.

He who breathes correctly appropriates intelligence and will from the sun. The freer his breathing the greater the degree of intelligent will. He who breathes freely acts freely. He who breathes deeply thinks deeply.

Only fear prevents free thought. Only restricted thought prevents free breathing.

Get rid of fear and you will need no teaching to breathe freely.

Thought and action are one. Every thought is action, but we are not yet trained to see the finer motions of thought; therefore we say, "thought sometimes prompts action"; not realizing that *all thought is motion, and all motion is thought*

One class of thinkers says breathing exercises are a necessity to a well-balanced mind and body. Another class says only thinking is necessary – the breathing will follow. Both are right, because *breathing is thinking and thinking is breathing.*

A man can no more breathe without thinking than he can think without breathing. The instant circulation of breath ceases, that instant there is no motion. No motion is annihilation.

A thinking exercise is a breathing exercise; a breathing exercise, or any other kind of an exercise, is a thinking exercise.

An exercise well done is one in which is put *all* the thought that it can contain; an exercise half done is one unwillingly, unintelligently done. The former is correct thinking; the latter is slovenly half thinking.

Somewhere away down in the animal kingdom we used to know how to breathe. That was before we learned to be scared at God and the devil – not to mention ourselves and other people. But by scare-thinking we developed the habit of half breathing. Half breathing is a habit of the human race. That is, on the male side. The female side lives on quarter breathing; because it has been taught to fear more things than men, and because women are more apt anyway at learning. Women have learned to shrink and lean. Not content with this, they have bound their feet and hands and laced themselves into strait jackets – the most infernal machine imaginable for squeezing the Solar Plexus out of all semblance to a radiating center, and shutting off the breath of life.

All this habit must be overcome in the only way possible – by the establishment of new habits; new habits of breathing, of thinking. Remember, breathing and thinking are *one.*

Therefore I say unto you, men and women, but especially women, *breathe.* And keep on breathing until you establish the habit of full, free breathing. You people who have been trying to think yourself into the free kingdom and who wonder why you seem to make so little progress, just set to work and breathe for dear life. That will help you as nothing else will. Just the very kind of thought we call "breathing" is the thought which frees from fear. The weak, sick, timid ones are the breathless ones. Asthmatics, consumptives and nervous folks need breath and plenty of it, to heal them. And they are the very ones who will not breathe if they can get out of it. They immure themselves in hot, airless rooms and gasp and gurgle and bewail fate; because they have been for years – for generations, perhaps – trying to get along without breath. This is their habit of thought.

Well, there is salvation – a new habit of thought. Practice breathing even half as diligently as you have practiced not breathing and you work out the salvation that is within you.

I will tell you just how to begin and just how to keep at it; and if you will practice faithfully for one short month you will be thoroughly convinced. And if you will keep at it until you have made full breathing a habit of thought you will be a new creature; sorrow and melancholy, fears and fighting will have ceased forever. Energy, ambition, power, joy will have grown up in their place; your shrunken and bent body will have straightened up; you will stand with a curve extra in the small of your back, instead of with one curve at the shoulders, such as you had when you were a monkey; you will walk with a spring, on the ball of the foot, instead of coming down on your heels or shuffling along any old way; your eyes will be bright and steady and ready to look kindly into every other pair of eyes; your mouth will be straight instead of drooping at the corners as in the old wailing days, and your lips will be soft and sweet to kiss; your skin will be fresh and clear and your voice will ring out, like bells over quiet waters, instead of being smothered in your throat and tinctured with whines or snarls as of old; in short, you will be a new being, born again of the "spirit" and ready to live and love and do.

Exercises

First and foremost, be sure you have plenty of open windows in your sleeping room; no a crack at top and bottom, but wide open windows. Use a screen to prevent draughts, if necessary.

When you wake in the morning throw everything wide open; lie flat on your back with outstretched arms and no pillow and light covering or, what is better, none at all. Relax from head to foot; close your mouth; take quietly a deep slow breath, filling the lungs evenly as possible all the way down; hold the breath as long as you can without straining; then see how very slowly and smoothly you can let the breath out. Pay very particular attention to this. See how slowly and steadily you can exhale the breath. Now, "get your breath" if you need to – as you certainly will if you are unaccustomed to deep breathing – and then do it over again. Repeat this five to seven times. Take about four seconds to inhale, eight seconds for holding, and as many as possible for exhaling. Possibly you cannot hold the breath so long at first; remember not to strain. Smooth, easy, steady – these are the first essentials. Practice will lengthen the breath. At first I could not inhale longer than two seconds, hold three and exhale three or four; and my heart beat as if I had exerted myself tremendously. It was three months before I could take five successive breaths such as I have described to you.

Right here I want to tell you what a help those three months of practice were to me in vocalizing. I was always troubled with short breath while singing. Four years of voice culture did little to help me. The three months in which I first practiced this breathing exercise it so happened that I was without a piano and never sang a note. Then one was brought into the house and I sang again. In spite of three or four months without a note of practice, I sang as I had never sung before. Never was singing such pleasure. It seemed to me I could sing any phrase, or two or three, with breath to spare and with a freedom I had never experienced before in my life. Since that time I have never known the old difficulty. I am convinced that systematic breathing exercises without vocalizing are of untold value to the singer.

If you are a man, or a woman who is sensible enough or slender enough to wear no corset, repeat this exercise two or three times each day, always in the same position and with the clothing loosened. And after retiring at night repeat again. Then command yourself to sleep quietly, breathe fully and wake refreshed at the usual hour.

If you will, in spite of all the medicos and Delsartes in the land, wear corsets, why, take the breathing exercises anyway. But take them standing, in the open air, if possible, or in an open window. Get a new, straight-front corset; let it out a notch or two more than you did the old one; after you put it on pull it a-way down in front and stand so your bustle is behind, where it belongs. Then throw your shoulders back, hold your head up, look like a sweet and gracious queen, turn your eyes toward heaven and all good, and breathe. Inhale love, power, shine, life – slowly, quietly; let it thrill you and permeate your every atom of being and fill your Solar Plexus with joy; let it transmute you and be transmuted; then lower your eyes, spread out your hands wide in blessing and breathe forth quietly, smoothly, slowly, all joys to all mankind.

If you are a man, never mind about the straight-front corset – just stand like an athlete, chest out and abdomen in, and take long, strong swigs from the sun; let them exhilarate all your being, souls and body; then breathe out blessings on the world. Take two or three breaths at each exercise; exercise several times a day, in standing position if you prefer; and recline night and morning for more breathing.

If you have a special pursuit in which you desire success, remember it when you are taking these exercises. While you are inhaling a breath you are negative, receptive; while you are holding the breath you are poised ready; while you are exhaling you are positive, radiant. You are giving out life to your dominion – to all who are less highly developed than yourself, to your environment in general, to your business, to whatsoever you are interested in. Then as you exhale a breath, spread forth your hands and breathe life into whatever you desire. You can grow friends, beautiful surroundings, money, loving thoughts, wisdom – anything *you will*, by this practice. I don't care two cents whether you have faith in it or not – just do it and you will find out that what I affirm is true.

The Solar Plexus is the seat of emotion. By proper exercise of the whole breathing apparatus you may gain such control of the Solar Plexus that anger, resentment, resistance, blues, discouragement and fear will be as foreign to you as are the awkward motions you used to make when you were first learning to walk or eat. All these unpleasant emotions are due to cramping the Solar Plexus. The exercises I have just given you will free the

Plexus and make you "feel good." Continued practice will establish the habit of "feeling good" – that is, the habit of feeling free.

Until you succeed in establishing a habit of feeling good you will have, as you have had heretofore, periods of depression. These will gradually grow less deep and be more readily dissipated. When you feel yourself growing depressed, for no matter what cause, break up the tendency as quickly as possible. Here is the way to do it:

Undress if possible; if not, loosen your clothing; lie down flat upon your back with arms outspread and without pillow; let go of everything mentally; inhale slowly through the nostrils a full breath; hold steady a second or two; then force the breath suddenly into the upper part of the lungs; hold there a second or two and then suddenly throw all the breath down as far as possible, at the same time exclaiming mentally to the Solar Plexus, "Wake up! Wake up!" Hold the breath down a second or two; then gradually let if flow back until the lungs are evenly filled again, hold an instant, and then see how very slowly and smoothly you can exhale the breath. Do this not over three times at one exercise and only when you are depressed. Then rise and move as if you were going somewhere and meant to get there. Get interested in what you have to do. The next time you think about your depression you will wonder what makes you feel so comfortable and full of quiet go. I have used this practice, which is my own discovery, for years; for all sorts of depressions from every imaginable cause; and never once has it failed to change my feelings entirely. It is guaranteed to cure anybody who will practice it with a will.

These directions sound complicated, but after a trial or two and a re-reading or two they will nearly do themselves, so easy and delightful will you find them and their effects. Never mind if your heart thumps a bit when you first attempt any breathing exercise. It would thump just the same after any new and vigorous exercise. Just be quiet and persist. Very shortly your hear will enter into the general enjoyment and keep as quiet as a summer morn, no matter how vigorously you force the breath up and down. This exercise properly persisted in will benefit or cure functional heart disease, as well as diseases of lungs and throat. In fact, there is hardly and ailment of the human frame which cannot be cured in this way, if the practice is kept up daily or oftener for a long enough period. Remember that the shine from your sun center is to your body what the shine from Old Sol is to plant life and planets; and these exercises establish in your solar center the habit of shining.

Chapter IV: Breathing Technique

There are breathers and breathers and breaths and breaths, and if you happen to be one kind of a breather you might take a good many thousand breaths without doing yourself very much good. All because you force one poor little bit of a muscle to do the work of a great man large muscles.

Perhaps some of you don't know that you have in your throat the neatest little trapdoor ever was seen. You might not know it is there, and you may never have heard its name, but I'll warrant you have experienced several unpleasant sensations in your day from having left this little trapdoor open at the wrong instant. And you have probably missed a great many enjoyable sensations by closing it up at unseasonable moments.

This neat little trapdoor, that works so smoothly you hardly knew you had it, is intended for just one purpose in ordinary life – the purpose of keeping anything more dense than ozone from getting into the air passage to the lungs.

But the epiglottis is a very intelligent and obedient little servant, and I have known singers to teach it to flap up and down very fast, and so help in producing staccato tones.

Then I have known other folks to impose shamefully upon this dainty little member of the human family, which is built for light, rapid motion and not for long strains.

Strange to say, it is the New Thought people, the disciples of love, who oftenest abuse it. But they don't mean to, of course.

These new thinkers have got hold somehow of the notion that there is great virtue in holding the breath a long time. So they pump themselves full of air and batten down that poor little trapdoor and keep it down until they get red in the face, and their hearts thump tempestuously and then go pit-a-pat.

Have you gone shopping recently in some big department store and had your ears assailed by a dreadful nasal wailing the while your eyes rested upon the legend, "Don't laugh – the pigs are dying?" And then you spied the pigs blown full of air and caterwauling themselves away. Whilst the pig is full and plugged up, the membrane of which it is made is stretched to the utmost. Now take him up between your two hands and squeeze him harder and harder. If there happens to be a weak spot he will burst. Or the plug may fly out. At any rate, you will stretch his skin, and it will take more air to make him plump again.

Now, that is just the way the wrong kind of holding the breath acts on your lungs. You stretch all the tissues of the lungs and batten down the epiglottis. Then the natural, untrained tendency of the chest and abdominal muscles being to straightway expel the air, all these muscles contract about your lungs, just as your fingers contracted about the skin pig, and the entire lung tissue and air passage, as well as the little trapdoor, are strained severely.

And this straining interferes with the circulation of the blood, reacting upon the heart, and, if there does happen to be a weak spot in the lungs, you invite a hemorrhage. To cap all this, you make the lung tissue flabby and lazy.

The lungs should never, in ordinary breathing exercises, be forced to hold air – not for one instant.

The lungs are a pair of bellows, which fill as the muscular walls are expanded.

It is not the forcing of air inward that expands the chest walls.

Expanding the chest and abdominal muscles draws in the air, making no more of a pressure inside the body than there is on the outside. This allows a free circulation of both air and blood, and permits perfect oxygenation.

It is not the lungs that need training to breathe. They always receive all the air that the muscles will give them room for.

And they remain expanded and free just as long as the muscles will permit.

Correct breathing is correct muscling.

Breathing practices should be muscle practices, with the trapdoor wide open from start to finish.

When you practice breathing never mind the breath. Just see how far, and evenly, you can expand your chest and abdominal muscles straight outward; how long you can hold them steadily there without pressure against the epiglottis, and how very slowly, evenly and softly you can contract those muscles again. Put your *will* into your muscles, where it belongs – put your attention into them – and you will get the knack of correct breathing.

Breathe always through the nostrils.

Don't try too hard. If you have to puff and blow after a long breath you made the divisions of that breath (inhaling, holding and exhaling) too long, and you shut the trapdoor. Try again. Breathe easily.

Breathe with a *purpose*. Did you know that the difference between a man and an idiot is the difference between a purpose and no purpose? The manliest man (woman included) is the one who has the deepest, highest, steadiest *purpose*.

The idiot breathes in short, irregular puffs, never once entirely filling or emptying his lungs! And his short, erratic little puffs go to build the thousand and one short, erratic little notions which make up his expressed self.

Aimless breathing practices are, like any other aimless efforts, beastly. Will your breath-generated power in a chosen direction. Aim with it. And see you aim high and steadily.

You can do anything you steadily purpose to do. Only vacillation can defeat you; — unless you should happen ignorantly to aim at something which would enslave the free will of another. For instance, I had a man write me once to "utterly subdue to him his wife, and make her obedient to him in all things!" Now, his wife used to be that kind of a goose, but she had positively outgrown it and left His Mightiness. And this man might breathe and speak the Word, and hire healers till crack o'doom, and that is all the good it would do him. You see he didn't aim high enough. If he had aimed to be sweet enough to win a woman's devotion, he could do it, though it might take a few more incarnations in his case. But he could get there in time. Or if he had aimed to be a successful artist, or writer, or business man, he could do it without fail, if he kept steadily at it. But he wanted to boss other folks, and other folks had sense enough to boss themselves.... I returned that man's money, and told him I gloried his wife's spunk.

Breathe rhythmically.

It is said a single dog trotting across a bridge will do more toward shaking it down than whole droves of draught horses and heavy loads. There is no rhythm to the motion of the dog.

It is said a man with a violin could shake down Brooklyn bridge by keeping up a steady vibration of the note the bridge is keyed to.

A rhythmical heart beat makes a powerful body.

Rhythmical breathing communicates rhythm to the heart and brain and gives the entire man a good time. Breathing regularly and deeply brings the whole body and brain and soul and spirit into harmony of action.

Harmony is health. Harmony is power.

Did you ever see four men, or women, take three or four long, even breaths in unison, and at the last inhalation raise with the tips of their fingers, a heavy man clear above their heads? Without those long, even breaths, that feat cannot be done.

Rhythmical breathing generates power in the body. During sleep the breathing is even and deep, and the body recuperates.

Recuperates from what? From the irregularity of action caused by the waking, the surface brain. The breathing apparatus responds to every conscious thought. It gasps with astonishment, stands still with fear, or puffs with excitement.

In the long, quiet night it recovers its natural rhythmic action.

Our breathing apparatus is like a child's untrained fingers – full of infinite capacity for the expression of beauty, harmony, power. But, like the child's fingers, our breathing apparatus needs training to work steadily, intelligently, even if the brain does get flighty or lazy. Just as each one of the child's individual fingers has to lean how to do its own work without responding to the impulsion sent to its mates, so the breathing apparatus must be taught to keep coolly, evenly at work no matter what is going on above in the brain or outside the body.

This can be accomplished by persistent practice.

Rhythmical action of the breathing machinery will keep the body full of power and prepare "a heart for any fate."

One who teaches his body to keep coolly, sweetly, harmoniously at work no matter what turns up, will cease to gasp and gurgle, faint and collapse at the very times he most needs power.

When you are "tired" or "discouraged" your body is starved by short, irregular breath supply.

Lie down flat, with arms out from the body and eyes closed. Inhale slowly, but not too slowly; just easily; as you inhale, say mentally, with eyes raised under your closed lids, "I am" – say it slowly and distinctly, and try quietly to realize that the Infinite is really you – "I and the Father are One." Keep the chest walls expanded for a moment and the throat open. Then slowly and very smoothly exhale the breath, lowering your eyes as you do so, under closed lids always, saying softly, lingeringly, mentally, with downward inflection, "Love." "I –am – Love."

Breathe rhythmically, as slowly as you can breathe easily, and always fully. Keep this up until your mind is quiet and you have forgotten all about being "discouraged" or "blue." Keep this up until I *am* consciousness has gone with the breath into the lungs, and so into the blood, and with it into all the body.

It takes about two minutes for the blood to make the circuit of the body. But in order to change your "feelings" it must make the circuit several times, setting up a new rhythmic vibration of *I – am – love* – consciousness. Your whole being must "catch" the vibrations of that grand, peaceful, powerful I *am* consciousness. Lungs, heart, solar center and brain must pulse together with the Infinite.

This is the best "concentration" exercise I know of – the only sure means I know of for becoming conscious of the power flowing outward from the "world *I am*: into the "world I do." It is the only *infallible* remedy I know for discouragement, unrest, lack of interest, impatience, anger, malice, revenge, resentment, and the hanging on habit. And I believe it to be literally infallible for any human being who really wants to be cured of any of these negatives.

Repeat the dose every time you feel negative. At first it may take ten minutes or more to free you, but after a time, five minutes will do it. If you nip every little spell in the bud, you will soon cease to feel distinctively negative at all.

In-breath the Infinite I *am*; let it renew you, mind and body; out-breathe Love, Wealth, all you desire. Remember, you do not take in things you desire – they press out through you. You in-breathe I am, Love, God.

Never mind what the trouble is – just chop it squarely off with the practice. Keep at it. There is simply no end to the good you will get out of it. You will practice it until you get your consciousness right with the real pulses of your being – the I *am* vibrations. In proportion as you live in that consciousness, you realize health, happiness, and *success*.

Whatever breathing practices you use or don't use, remember to straighten up and take a few, full, slow breaths, whenever you think of it – no matter where you are or what you are doing. There is *life* in it and Joy.

Faith By Katherine Quinn

I sent Desire across the sea.
('Twas years and years ago)
I gave the lad what gold I had,
And vowed through weal or woe

That I'd be true unto my love
Until his journey's end,
And that each day he was away
A message I would send.
My friends all smiled to see my faith.

Then sighed, "Alack, alack,
Your only gains will be your pains,
For he will ne'er come back."
I paid no heed unto their words,
But worked on steadfastly.

When worst I fared, most loud declared
That I had ships at sea.
Last night my vessel touched on shore;
And Peace sat in her bow.
And Joy was there, and Love most fair.

And Plenty strode her prow.
Desire had brought them all to me
Across the briny foam.
"Ah, well-a-day," my friends now say,
"Who'd think that he'd come home?"

Happiness and Marriage

Table of Contents:

The inner side of every cloud Is bright and shining;
I therefore turn my clouds about,
And always wear them inside out— To show the lining.
                    —James Whitcomb Riley

And I will show that there is no imperfection in the present,
    and can be none in the future,
And I will show that whatever happens to anybody it may be
    turned to beautiful results.
                    —Walt Whitman

Chapter I: To Be Happy Though Married

"Some dear relatives of mine proposed Ada as my future bride. I like Ada and I gladly accepted the offer, and I mean to wed her about the middle of this year. Is this a working of the Law of Attraction? I want to make our married life happy and peaceful. I long for a wedded life of pure blessedness and love and joy without even a pinhead of bitterness ever finding lodgment in our household. How can I attain this state of peace? This is what I now do: I enter into the Silence daily at a particular hour and enjoy the mental picture of how I desire to be when married. Am I right? Please tell me how to make my ideal real." Tudor, Island of Ceylon.

The above letter comes from a member of the Success Circle who is a highly cultured and interesting looking native East Indian. We have a full length photo of him in native costume.

He asks if "this is the working of the Law of Attraction." Certainly it is. Just as the sun acts through a sheet of glass so the Law of Attraction acts through the conventionalities of a race. Whatever comes together is drawn together by the Law. Whatever is held together is held by that same Law of Attraction.

This is just as true in unhappy marriages as in happy ones. If two people are distinctly enough individualized; that is, if they understand and command themselves sufficiently; their attraction and marriage will bring to them only pleasure. If they are not distinctly enough individualized there will be a monkey-and-parrot experience whilst they are working out the wisdom *for which they were attracted.*

When soda and sour milk are drawn together there is a great stew and fizz, but the end thereof is sweetness and usefulness. So with two adverse and uncontrolled natures; but out of the stew comes added wisdom, self-command and rounded character for each.

When each has finished the work of helping the other to develop they will either find themselves *really* in love with each other, or they will fall apart. *Some stronger attraction will separate them at the right time*—perhaps through divorce, perhaps through death.

All our goings and comings are due to the Law of Attraction. The Law of Attraction giveth, and it taketh away. *Blessed* is the Law. *Let* it work. And forget not that *all* things are due to its working.

This does not mean that the Law has no way of working *except* through the conventionalities of a people. Many times the attraction is to break away from the conventional. *The stronger attraction always wins*— whatever is, is *best* for *that time and place.*

"Tudor" says he "enters into the silence daily at a particular hour and enjoys the mental picture of how he desires to be when married."

His success all depends upon the *equity* in that picture; upon its truth to the law of being.

An impractical idealist lives in the silence with beautiful pictures of "how he desires to be when married." When he gets married there isn't a single detail of his daily experience which is like his mental picture. He is sadly disappointed and perhaps embittered or discouraged.

It all depends upon the picture. If Tudor's picture contains a benignant lord and master and a sweet little Alice Ben Bolt sort of wife who shall laugh with delight when he gives her a smile and wouldn't hurt his feelings for a farm; who does his bidding before he bids and is always content with what he is pleased, or able, to do for her; if this is the style of Tudor's mental picture he is certainly doomed to disappointment.

I have a suspicion that Tudor is a natural born teacher. His mental pictures may represent himself as a dispenser of moral and mental blessings. He may see Ada sitting adoringly at his feet, ever eager to learn. If so there will certainly be disappointment. East Indian girls may be more docile than American girls; East Indian men may be better and wiser lords and masters; but "Ada" is a Human Being before she is an East Indian; and a Human Being instinctively revolts from a life passed in leading strings. If Tudor continues to remind her that he is her schoolmaster she will certainly revolt; inwardly if not outwardly. Whether the revolt comes inwardly or outwardly harmony is doomed.

The first principle of happy marriage is *equality*. The second principle is *mutual confidence*, which can *never* exist without the first.

I do not mean by "equality" what is usually meant. One member of the married twain may be rich, the other poor in worldly goods; one an aristocrat, the other plebeian; one educated, the other unschooled; and yet they may be to each other what they are in *truth*, equals.

Equality is a *mental state*, not a matter of birth or breeding, wisdom or ignorance. The *truth* is that *all* men and women are equal; all are sparks of the One Life; all children of the one highly aristocratic "Father"; all heirs to the wisdom and wealth of the ages which go to make up eternity.

But all men and women are more or less unconscious, in spots at least, of this truth. They spend their lives "looking down" upon each other. Men "look down" upon their wives as "weak" or "inferior," and women look down upon their husbands as "animals" or "great brutes." Men are contemptuous of their wives visionariness, and women despise their husbands for "cold and calculating" tendencies.

Every man and woman values certain qualities highly, and in proportion as another fails to manifest these particular qualities he is classed as "low," and his society is not valued.

This is the great source of trouble between husbands and wives. Each values his or her own qualities and despises the other's. So *in their own minds* they are not equal, and the first principle of harmony is missing.

The real truth is that in marriage a man is schoolmaster to his wife *and she is equally schoolmistress to him*. This is true in a less degree, of *all* the relationships of life.

The Law of Attraction draws people together *that they may learn*.

There is but one Life, which is growth in wisdom and knowledge.

There is but one Death, *which is refusal to learn*.

If husbands and wives were equals *in their own minds* they would not despise each other and *refuse to learn* of each other.

The Law of Attraction, or Love, almost invariably attracts opposites, and for their own good. A visionary, idealistic woman is drawn to a practical man, where, kick and fuss and despise each other as they will, she is bound to become more practical and he more idealistic. They exchange qualities in spite of themselves; each is an unconscious agent in rounding out the character and making more abundant the life of the other.

Much of this blending of natures is accomplished through passion, the least understood of forces. And the children of a union of opposites, even where there is *great* contempt and unhappiness between the parents, are almost invariably *better balanced* than *either* of the parents.

I cannot believe that unhappy marriages are "mistakes" or that they serve no good purpose. The Law of Attraction draws together those who need each other at that particular stage of their growth. The unhappiness is due to their own foolish *refusal* to learn; and this refusal is due to their contempt for each other. They are like naughty children at school, who cry or sulk and refuse to work out their problems. Like those same naughty children they *make themselves* unhappy, and fail to "pass" as soon as they might.

Remember, that contempt for each other is at the very bottom of all marital unhappiness. The practical man despises his wife's impulsive idealism and tries to make her over. The wife despises his "cold and calculating" tendencies and tries to make him over. That means war, for it is impossible to make over *anybody but yourself*.

Because the man despises his wife's tendencies and she despises his, it never occurs to either to try making over *themselves*, thus helping along the very thing they were drawn together for.

If Tudor's picture holds two people who are *always* equal though utterly different; whose future actions are an unknown quantity to be taken as they come and each action to be met in a spirit of *respect* and inquiry, with a view to understanding and learning from it; if over and through all his picture Tudor spreads a glow of *purpose* to preserve *his own* respect and love *for her*, at all costs;—if this is the sort of picture Tudor makes in the silence he will surely realize it later.

It requires but one to strike the keynote of respect and personal freedom in marriage; the other will soon come into harmony.

You can readily see that all marital jars come from this lack of equality in the individual mind. If a man thinks he is perfectly able to take care of and to judge for himself he resents interference from another. On the other hand if he believes his wife is equally able to judge for *herself*, he *never* thinks of interfering with her actions. Of course the same is true of the wife. It is lack of respect and confidence which begets the making-over spirit in a family, and from this one cause arises all in harmony.

Individual freedom is the *only* basis for harmonious action; not only in marriage but in all other relationships of life.

And individual freedom *cannot* be granted by the man or woman who considers his or her judgments superior to the judgments of another. A man *must* accord his wife *equal* wisdom and power with himself, else he *cannot* free her to act for herself. A woman must accord her husband that same equality, or she *cannot* leave him free.

It is human (and divine) nature to correct what we believe to be wrong. Only in believing that the other "king (or queen) can do no wrong," lies the possibility of individual freedom, in marriage or out.

The man or woman who knows he or she is believed in and trusted is very careful to *deserve* that trust. Did you know that? The sure way to have your wishes consulted is to exalt and appreciate the other party. Did you know that a man or woman will cheerfully sacrifice his or her own opinions in order to retain the respect and love of the other? But if he thinks the respect and love of the other party is growing less he will give free reign to his own desires.

Married people "grow apart" for the one reason that they find fault with each other. Of course it begins by their being disrespectful to each other's faults, but it soon develops into disrespect of each other. From "looking down" upon a husband's faults it is only a few short steps to looking down upon *him*. His faults keep growing by recognition, and his good points keep shrivelling for lack of notice, until *in your mind* there is nothing left but faults. From trying to make him over you come to despair, and give him up as an altogether bad job.

And there isn't a grain of sense in all this madness. Stick to the *truth* and you will get rid of the madness and the friction, too. The truth is that your husband, or your wife, would be an egregious *fool* to follow your judgments. You don't know beans from barley corn when it comes to the actions of anybody but yourself. The One Spirit which enlightens *you* as to *your* actions is also enlightening your other half as to *her* actions; and do you suppose this Spirit is going to favor *you* with better judgment about your other half's duties, than it has given *her?* I guess *not*. Don't be presumptuous, my boy. Do you own little best, and *trust* your other half to do hers. Trust that she *is* doing the best.

And above all trust the One Spirit to run you both.

If you do this your wife will *rise fast* in your esteem. And the higher she finds herself in your esteem the harder she will try to please you— and rise higher.

And, girls, don't forget that the shoe fits equally well the other foot. Either man or wife can bring harmony out of chaos simply by *respecting* the other half *and all his or her acts*.

A marriage without "even a pinhead of bitterness" is a marriage without a pin-point of fault-finding, mental or oral.

Chapter II: A Tale of Woe

"Why is it that, in more than two-thirds of families the wife and mother bears not only the children but the burdens and heartaches? The husband supplies the *money* (generally not enough), the wife has the care of a growing and increasing family, the best of everything is saved for 'Father' and he is waited on, etc. If the children annoy him he goes to his club; if the wife dies, why there are plenty more women for the asking. Thousands of women are simply starving for Love and men are either willfully blind or wholly and utterly selfish. You possibly know that this is quite true. Another thing that has caused me many a time to question everything: During the Christmas holidays many times I have seen half-clad, hungry, shivering little ones gazing longingly into the wonderful show windows, wanting probably just one toy, while children no more worthy drive by in carriages, having more than they want. Love, home, mother, everything; on the other hand hunger, want, blues (many times), and both God's children. Let us hear what you have to say about this." B. B.

Why does the mother in two-thirds of the families bear not only the children but the burdens and heartaches? *Because she is too thoughtless and inert not to.* It is *easier* to submit to bearing children than it is to rise up and take command of her own body. It is easier to carry burdens than to wake up and *fire* them. It is easier to "bear" things and grumble than it is to kick over the traces and *change* them. To be sure, most women are yet under the hypnotic spell of the old race belief that it is woman's duty to "submit" herself to any kind of an old husband; but that is just what I said—women find it easier to go through life half asleep rather than to *think* for themselves. Paul says a woman is *not* to think, she is to ask her husband to think for her. (At least that is what the translators *say* Paul says. Privately, I have my suspicions that those manly translators helped Paul to say a bit more than he meant to.) It is *easier* to let her husband think for her even when she doesn't like his thoughts. So she uses her brain in *grumbling* instead of thinking.

People who don't think are ruled by *feeling*. Women feel. They feel not only for themselves but for other people. They shoulder the burdens of the whole family and a few outside the family. They do it themselves— because it is *easier* to feel than to think. Nobody walks up to a woman and says, "Here—I have a burden that's very heavy—*you* carry it whilst I go off and have a good time." No. The woman simply *takes* the burden and hugs it and "feels" it—and *prides herself on doing it.* And maybe the thing *she* hugs as a burden is no burden at all to the other people in the family. My dear, women as a rule are chumps. They'd rather feel *anything* than to *think* the right thing.

Now I'd like to know if you think a woman who has made herself round-shouldered and wrinkled and sour-visaged over burdens—*anybody's* burdens, real or fancied—is such a creature as attracts love or consideration from *anybody*. Of course she is not. It is no wonder she receives no love or consideration from her husband or anybody else. She has made a pack mule out of herself for the carrying of utterly useless burdens that nobody *wants* carried and the carrying of which benefits nobody; and now that she has grown ugly and sour at the business she need not feel surprised at being slighted. And she need not blame folks for slighting her. *She* assumed the burdens; she carried them; *she* wore herself out at it; it is all her own fault. It was *easier* for her to feel, and grumble, than to wake up and *think*, and change things.

Nobody who *thinks* will carry a single burden for even a single day. He knows that fretting and worrying and grumbling only *double the burden* and accomplish nothing.

Woman has *built herself* for bearing children and burdens. When she gets tired of her bargain she will *think her way out of the whole thing*. In the meantime the harder the burdens grow the more quickly she will revolt and make of herself something besides a burden bearer.

It is all nonsense to talk about the men being "willfully blind or wholly and utterly selfish." No man *wants* a burden-bearing, round-shouldered, wrinkled and fagged-out wife. No man respects or loves a woman who will "submit" to bearing unlimited burdens or babies either. And if a woman "submits" and yet keeps up a continual grumbling and nagging about it, a man simply despises her.

What every man *hopes* for when he marries a woman, is that she will be a bright, trim, *reasonable comrade*. If she is even half-way that she will get all the love and consideration she can long for. But in three-quarters of the cases of marriage the woman degenerates into a whining bundle of *thought-less feelings* done up in a slattern's dress and smelling like a drug-shop. Her husband in despair gives up trying to understand her, or to love her either.

The woman in such a case is apt to suffer most. Why not? *She makes it the business of her life to "suffer."* She *prides* herself on how much she has had to "suffer," and "bear." She cultivates her "feelings" to the limit. A man thinks it "unmanly" to *give way* to "feelings." So he uses all his wits to keep from doing so, and to enable him to hide his own disappointment and make the best of life as he finds it.

A man uses his best *judgment* when he meets disappointment. A woman trots out her "feelings" and her best pocket-handkerchief, and calls in the neighbors. So the woman gets the lion's share of "sympathy"—which means that all the other women get out *their* best handkerchiefs and try to imagine just how *they* would "feel" if in her place.

Of course there *are* exceptions. I *have* heard of men who wept and retailed their woes; and I have heard of women with gumption.

The woman who wrote the letter at the head of this chapter is a feel-er, not a thinker. She looks at the forlorn, bedraggled specimens of her own sex and "*feels*" with them, never *thinking* that the women themselves have anything to do with making their conditions. She "feels" with the woman because *she* is a woman. Being an unthinking creature she cannot "feel" for the man at all.

Woman is the weaker creature for no other reason than that she lives in her "feelings."

Man is the stronger for no other reason than that he uses his wits and his will to *control* his feelings. "B. B." has seen children gazing into shop windows. Immediately she imagines how *she* would "feel" if in their places. She does not stop to *think* that in all probability the simple act of gazing into the window may bring more real joy to those children than the *possession* of the whole windowful of toys would bring to some rich man's child. She does not *think* that life consists not in possessions or environment, but in the *ability to use* possessions or environment. If she were an Edwin Abbey or a Michael Angelo she would gaze on our chromo-bedecked walls and work herself up into a great state of "feeling" because we had to have such miserable daubs instead of real works of art. If she saw us gazing on an Abbey or Angelo picture she would weep tears to think we couldn't have such pictures instead of those hideous bright chromos on our walls. It would never occur to her that we might be privately comparing her Abbeys and Angelos with our chromos, *and wondering how anybody could possibly see beauty in the Abbeys and Angelos.*

About nine-tenths of women's so-called "sympathy" is just about as foolish and misplaced as that. If "B. B." would go up and get acquainted with some of those small youngsters she sees gazing into the shop windows she would find some of her illusions dispelled. She would find among them less "longing" than she thinks, and more wonder and criticism and pure curiosity—such as she would find in her own heart if she were gazing at a curio collection.

I remember a large family of very small boys that I used to "feel" for, very deeply. Poor little pinched, ragged looking fellows they were, and always working before and after school hours. I gave them nickels and dimes and my children's outgrown clothes, and new fleece lined gloves for their blue little hands. They kept the clothes hung up at home and the gloves stuffed in their pants pockets. And one day I discovered that every one of those small youngsters had a *bank account*—something I had never had in my life! They lived as they *liked* to live, and I had been harrowing my feelings and carrying their (?) burdens for nothing.

This world is *not* a pitiful place. It is a lovely great world, full of all sorts of people, every one of whom *exactly fits into* his conditions.

And the loveliest thing of all about this bright, blessed old world is that there is not a man, woman or child in it who cannot *change* his environment if he doesn't like the one he now occupies. He can *think* his way into anything.

A real, deep, tender feeling will prompt one to do all he can to alleviate distress or add to the world's joy. *Real* feeling prompts to action. But this sentimental slush which slops over on anything and everything in general is nothing but an imitation of the real thing. To sympathize to the extent of *acting* is good; to harrow up the feelings when you cannot or will not act, is simply weakness.

"Feeling" is subject to the same law as water. Take away its banks and it spreads all over creation and becomes a stagnant slough of despond. Confine it by banks of *common-sense* and *will* and it grows deep and tender and powerful, and bears blessings on its bosom.

The professional pityer is adding to the sum total of the world's misery.

The world is like "sweet Alice Ben Bolt"; it laughs with delight when you give it a smile, and gets out its pocket handkerchief to weep with you when you call it "Poor thing!"

Then it cuts its call short and runs around the corner to tell your neighbor what a tiresome old thing you are anyway.

Never you mind the tribulations you can't help, dearie. Just wake up and *be* the brightest, happiest, sweetest thing you know how to be, and the world will-be that much better off.

Chapter III: To Be Loved

"I desire to attract love from the Infinite or somewhere, that I may not be starved for it, as I have been ever since I married. My husband sneers at the New Thought, and in fact at nearly all that is best in me."

Caroline.

And yet this woman has children to love her. She thinks she is in need of being loved; but what she really needs is *to love*. Being loved is the *effect* of loving. A loving man or woman can never want for love. Others turn to them in love as naturally as flowers turn to the sun.

In order to be loved you must *radiate* love. Instead of trying to attract the love of others, seek to *give* your love to others, *expecting nothing in return*. After a time you will find the unexpected coming to you spontaneously.

Learn to love by loving *all* people and *things*, and especially all things you find to do.

This same Caroline wants to "rise above drudgery." What *is* drudgery? *It is simply unloved work*—nothing more nor less. *Any* work which is looked down upon, and which is done with the hands *whilst the heart and mind are criticizing it*, and running out after other things,—*any* work thus done is drudgery. Work done with the hands *and a small and unwilling part* of the mind, is drudgery. To her who *respects*, and *loves*, and does with a will what she finds to do, there is no drudgery.

Let the woman who longs to be loved begin to *love*, by practicing on her work. To quit calling it "drudgery"; to put *all* her mind and will and *soul* into *each* piece of work as it comes; is the first and longest step toward loving it. It is an easily demonstrated fact that we learn to love anything we persist in doing with a whole-souled will.

To love our work enlarges our capacity for loving people, and the more we love people, *and the more people we love*, the more radiant we become.

It is the radiant lover whom all the world loves. Do you know that love and the lack of love are governed by "auto-suggestion"? It is *natural* to love, as every child does. But as we grow up we keep saying to ourselves (this is auto-suggestion, you know) that we "don't like this," and we "don't like that," until really we *shut up* our love and live in a continual state of "don't like"—a state which in due time develops into *hate*—hate for self as well as others. "Don't like" does it all.

Now *cultivate* love by auto-suggestion. Keep saying, "I *like* this," and "I like that." *Hunt* for things to like, and even tell yourself you like things when you don't *feel* that you like them at all.

Feeling is a *result* of suggestion. Nothing easier to prove than that. A hypnotist can, by suggestion, make you feel almost anything, whether it is true or not. He will say, "You feel sad," and straightway you will feel so. Then he will say, "You feel happy," and you do. Your feelings are like a harp, and your *statements*, or auto-suggestions, are the fingers which pick the strings.

Take good care to play the tunes you *want*—to say you *like* things, or love them. Then you will quickly respond and *feel* that you like or love them. Keep *practicing* until you love *all* the time. Then you will *be* loved to your heart's content.

Chapter IV: The Pharisee Up-To-Date

As long as you continue to hug the delusion that you are "not to blame" for the unpleasant things in your conditions you might just as well profess the old thought as the new. The very fundamental principle of mental science is the statement that *man is a magnet and able to attract what he will*. To repudiate this statement is to knock the props out from under the whole philosophy. Better stay an old-thoughter and let Jesus suffer for your sins and those of your relatives and friends. At least Jesus *took* the sins of the world to bear, all of his own free will. There is some comfort in letting Jesus do what he chose to do.

But you have turned away from Jesus as a scapegoat. You refuse to lay your burdens on him who offered to bear them; and you refuse to bear them yourself. Instead you distribute them around among your relations and friends and then fret your soul because they won't accept your distributions. Of course you excuse yourself by acknowledging "your share of responsibility" for the unpleasantness of conditions, but if you will examine carefully you will find that your portion of the responsibility includes most of the *good* things in your conditions, whilst you have portioned off almost *all* the responsibility for the *bad* things among your protesting—or indifferent—relatives. You always say, "*I* try so hard," but you never balance that with, "*He* tries so hard,"—"*They* try so hard." You get all the I-try-items in your own pile and the don't-try-items in other folk's piles. "*If* it were not for Tom and Dick and Harry and Fan you would do wonders—*if* they'd only treat you with *half* the consideration other people give you, or half *they* give other people!—*if!—if!*"

I wonder why they don't indeed! It is just because you are you, *and you attract your own particular kind of treatment*. To all intents and purposes Tom, Dick, Harry and Fan are a punch and Judy show and *you pull the strings*. When other people pull the strings there's a different sort of show. *You* are the motive power in *all their treatment of you*. Not a tone or look or act of theirs in your direction but *you* are responsible for; it was *you* and no other who drew them to you; and it is you and no other who hold them there.

Now don't say, "I don't see *how!*" Of course not—*you haven't wanted to see how*—you've been too intent justifying yourself. And anyway, it takes an open mind, and some time, and much *faith* to enable us to see the *principles* of things. We have to *act* as if they were so, a long time before we see that they are. If you had *acted* upon the principle that you are a magnet and that *all* that comes to you comes by your attraction, you'd have long ago had your eyes opened to "see how." And you'd have made progress and *changed your conditions*.

If you are ever going to be a magnet you are one now. If you are ever going to be able to attract to the hair's breadth whatsoever you will *then you are doing it now*. There will be no miraculous change in the running gear of this universe to enable you to attract what you want.

What you now are in essence and working principle you have always been, and you will always be—the same yesterday, today and forever—a self-made magnet, *working to the hair's breadth.*

Only by Changing the Quality of Your Magnetism Can You Change Your Environment and Attract Different Treatment from Tom, Dick, Harry and Fan.

Sweetness within brings sweetness without. You have been more or less bitter and self-justifying within, and Tom, Dick, Harry and Fan have danced to the strings you pulled.

As long as you think *you* try and they don't; as long as you think *your* judgment superior to theirs; *your* ideals loftier and worthier; *your* ways better; you will get from them responses of carelessness, bitterness, lack of consideration, selfishness.

You are inconsiderate of *their* ideas, ideals, judgments and ways; *in self-preservation* they are inconsiderate of yours. If you had your way they'd be pretty little putty images of *your* ideals, judgments, wishes, ways and feelings. The Law of Individuality prevents your imposing yourself on them. You think you are finding fault with *their* "lack of consideration"; *you are really condemning the law of being.*

If you are ever to be a magnet you are one *now. All* that comes *is* "your fault." If anything different comes it will come through *your* change of mental attitude and action.

It will not do to throw it on "Karma" either, and say you are receiving now the unpleasant things deserved in a previous state of existence. The mills of the gods grind slowly but they are not so dead slow as all that. What you thought and did in a previous state has determined your parentage and childhood environment in this. But the pangs you suffer today have their roots in yesterday or day before, or the year before that. Cause and effect trip close upon each other's heels—so close that the careless or ignorant observer misses the trip. He exaggerates the *effect* if it be an unhappy one, and goes nosing for a bigger cause than the real one. How could *his* little slip of this morning, or yesterday, be the cause of this *terrible* evil which has befallen him?—and he slides completely over the real cause. *And keeps on repeating it.*

Self-righteousness, by blinding your eyes to the truth, is the direct cause of the most gigantic and the most subtle miseries of the world. These awfully good people who fully realize how hard they have always tried to do right, are the unhappiest people in the world—unless I except Tom, Dick, Harry and Fan, the victims of these self-righteous reformers. No, I can't even except these; for they at least generally succeed in having their own way in spite of the would-be reformer. But what so utterly disheartening as continued *lack of success*? And the self-righteous one never succeeds. It is hard, *hard*, to be so wise and willing, with such *high* ideals (the self-righteous one is strong on ideals), and *never* to succeed in making Tom, Dick and Harry conform to them. Do you see why Jesus said so often, "Woe comes to the Pharisee" —the self-righteous? And why he called them hypocrites? Of course they are unconscious of their hypocrisy—self-righteousness blinds them to the truth; they think *others* are to blame for most of the self-righteous one's own hard conditions.

The self-righteous one is doomed to a tread-mill of petty failures. He goes round and round his own little personal point of view and learns nothing.

It is by getting at the *other fellow's* point of view that we learn things—about him and ourselves, too. When the self-righteous one wakes up to the *fact* that the world is *full* of people whose points of view are *just exactly* as right and wise and ideal as his own; and begins to *feel with*, and *pull with* these other people, instead of against them; when he does this he will find himself out of the treadmill to *stay*. As he shows a disposition to consider *other* people's ideals and help others in the line *they* want to go, he will find the whole world eager to help *him* in the way *he* wants to go. The self-righteous one works alone and meets defeat. The one who, recognizing his own righteousness *in intent*, yet forgets not that *others are even as he,* is the true friend and *be*-friended, of all the world.

Now don't let this homily slip off *your* shoulders. We are *all* self-righteous in spots, and none of us is so *very* wise that he cannot by self-examination and readjustment learn a lot more.

Each soul *in its place* is wisest and best. Don't *you* try to get into the pilot house and steer things for Tom, Dick, or Harry. Stay in your own and steer clear of the rocks of anger, malice, revenge, *resentment, resistance, interference* and *immoderation*.

Chapter V: So near and Yet So Far

"Help me to make things go forward instead of backward. I want to be neat and attractive, with a good head of hair, a good complexion and good health. I want to help my husband so he will fall in love with me to make home beautiful, attractive and comfortable. I want bright eyes and freedom from that careworn look. Oh, I want to draw my husband nearer to me." (From a Taurus woman, aged twenty-seven.)

Isn't that pitiful? And heaven knows—or ought to—how many poor women, *and men, too*, live with that same dumb longing to get nearer and be chums with somebody. That cry touches my heart, for I lived years in the same state.

And, oh, how I struggled to draw others nearer to me. How I agonized and cried and prayed over it. How I worked to make home attractive. How I cooked and washed and scrubbed, sewed and patched and darned to please! How I quickly brushed my hair and hustled into a clean dress so as to be neat and ready when my husband came in! And how I ached and despaired inwardly because he frowned and found fault! How I studied books of advice to young wives! How their advice failed! How I *tried* and *tried* to get him to confide in me and make a chum of me! And how the more I tried the more he had business downtown! Oh, the growing despair of it all! And the growing illnesses, too! Oh, the gulf that widened and widened between us! Oh, the *loneliness*! Oh, the *uselessness* of life!

I *had* to give it up. I wasn't enough of a hanger-on to sink into a state of perpetual whining protest, or to commit suicide. When I was finally *convinced* that I *couldn't* draw him nearer I gave it up and began to take notice again, *of other things*. I *let* him live his life and I took up the *"burden"* of my own "lonely" existence.

And the first thing I knew my "burden" had grown *interesting*, and I was *no longer lonesome*. I began to live my life to *please myself*, instead of living it for the purpose of *making over* the life of another.

The *next* thing I knew my husband didn't have so much business downtown, and he had more things he wanted to tell me. I found we were nearer than I ever dreamed we'd be.

You see, I had become *more comfortable to live with*. I had quit *trying* to draw him nearer, and behold, *he was already near*.

In the old days I lived strenuously. I hustled so to get the house and the children and myself *just so*, that I got *my aura* into a regular snarl. My husband being a healthy animal, felt the snarl before he saw the immaculateness; and like any healthy animal he snarled back—and had business downtown. He responded to my *real* mental and emotional state, responded against his will many times; and I did not know it. I supposed him perverse and impossible of pleasing. I *knew I* had tried my best (according to my lights, which it had not occurred to me to doubt), but it never entered my cranium that *he* had tried, too. I looked upon the outward appearance—my immaculate appearance, met by fault-finding or indifference I Poor me! Perverse he!

Poor Martha, troubled about many things, when only one thing is needful—a quiet mind and faithful soul. History does not state if Martha had a husband. If she did, he was perpetually downtown. And Jesus preferred Mary, the Comfortable One, to Martha. Poor lonesome Martha! And she tried *so hard* to please.

I used to know a woman who never did a thing but look sweet. She was pretty and sympathetic and *cheery*. Her husband and six children idolized her, and fairly fell over themselves to please her and keep the home beautiful for her. There was physical energy galore lavished *gladly* by the family, in doing what is commonly considered the mother's work.

And there was apparently nothing whatever the matter with that woman, who was always sweet and pretty as a new blown rose, and looked not a day over twenty. She was simply born tired and wouldn't work. Of course the neighbors said things about her; but nobody *could* say things *to* such a sweet tempered, cordial and pretty woman. And there'd have been razors flying through the air if anybody had dared hint to that husband or one of those children that mother was anything less than perfection. The family explanation was that "mother is not strong."

But that mother did more for that family than all the others put together. *She made the atmosphere*, and she was the life-giving sun around which husband and children revolved, and from which they received the real Light of Life—the power which develops the good in us.

The mother's main business in life was that of *appreciating*. She was the confidante, the counselor, the optimistic teacher, and the appreciative audience for six children and a husband, besides a lot of neighbors who carried their troubles to her. She performed more mental work than it takes to manage a billion dollar trust. She kept six children, not only out of mischief, but *happily busy* at all sorts of household and outdoor work which it was well for them to know. They learned to keep house and farm by keeping them, whilst she sat by and enthused and directed their efforts. She made them *love* it all. She helped them over the hard places in their school work and enthused them to do better work. They carried off the school prizes under her admiring eyes, and ran straight to lay them in her lap and receive that proud and happy smile of hers.

Her husband worked like a slave *with the heart of a king*. She thought him the best, bravest, brightest of men, and told him so a dozen times a day, besides *looking* it every time he came in range of her big, loving brown eyes and smooth, rosy cheeks.

I never heard of an unkind word in that family, and those six children grew up into splendid young manhood and womanhood. Their mother is still the blessed sun of their existence. She is prettier, healthier and happier now, and so proud of her fine children.

And she is *up-to-date*. She has studied and read with her whole family and is interested with them in the world's present events, art, literature and religion.

Do you think that woman ever complains of loneliness, or "tries so hard" to draw husband or children "nearer"? No. She long ago chose the "one thing needful"—*a faith-full heart*. Her physical strength would not bear much strain without depressing her faith-full-ness; therefore she left the physical labor out, *as less important*. To her the *Life* was more than meat or raiment, so she ministered to the Life—to the joy of living. A stronger woman, physically, could have ministered more efficiently to the physical side without neglecting the "one thing needful." This woman chose the better part and stuck to it; and *results* prove her righteousness.

The foolish woman looketh upon the outward appearance and is troubled over *many* things. She wears herself out trying to keep the *outside* immaculate and grieves her heart out because she misses the one thing of great price, the *joy of loving and being loved, of trusting and being trusted.*

Do you know that we are *never* far away from *anybody?* We are close, *so close* to our husbands; our children; our friends; *even to our enemies if we have them;* and to those we never saw or heard of. *We are all One. Your* soul is *my soul too.* Only our bodies are at all separated, and they are separated *only as the harbor is separated from the sea.* Our bodies are but inlets of One Great Soul; and they are but the smallest part of ourselves. Is it then not foolish to *try* to draw another nearer? Why, we are *now* so near we *can't* be nearer; we are *One.* Why strive to do what is *already* done?

Ah, you see, we work from a false hypothesis. We are so concerned with the many things on the *outside* that we lose sight of *inside truths.*

Take your husband's nearness for granted. Be not troubled over the many things of appearance. *Have faith in him.* If there is any "drawing nearer" to be done see that *you* draw near to him *in faith and love.* Instead of mentally or verbally sitting down on his motives, words or acts, *try to feel as he does, that you may understand him.*

As we geow in understanding of another we grow in love and realization of our nearness to that one. In proportion as we dislike or are repelled by any person or his actions, in that proportion we fail to understand him.

As one human being is revealed to another the sense of nearness grows. Now do you imagine that distrust and censure will help a soul reveal itself? Of course not. But if you can be comfortable and indulgent to a man, and especially if you can cultivate a real admiring confidence in him, he will unfold his very heart of hearts to you. It is *you* who must come near in faith and love, if you would find your husband near to you.

To sum up:

1. You and your husband *are* close together—so close you are *One.*

2. If you would *feel* the truth of this you must come to your husband in faith-full love, and you *must not allow yourself* to condemn or judge, verbally or mentally, his revelations of himself. You must vibrate *with* him where you can, and *keep still in faith* where you can't understand him and meet him.

3. You must persist in thus doing, until faith and love and understanding become the habit of your life.

4. The same rules apply if you would feel your nearness to any other person, *or to all persons.*

Every man is in embryo a good and thoughtful and loving husband. A wise wife will give him the loving, full-of-faith, appreciative atmosphere which encourages development.

"We are all just as good as we know how to be, and as bad as we dare be." *And we are all growing better.* Why not chant the beauties of the good instead of imagining it our "duty" to eternally bark against the bad?

It is said there cannot be a model husband without a model wife, and *vice versa.* True. Then if yours is not a model husband *don't assume that you are a model wife fitted to judge and admonish him.*

Be still and get acquainted with him.

Make it your *first* object in life to cultivate a serene and faith-full heart and aura.

As a means toward this end cultivate a *full* appreciation of whatever and whoever comes near you. Cultivate the spirit of praise; and *trust* where you cannot see.

Second, take *good* care of your body and personal appearance. Allow plenty of time for bathing, caring for your hair, nails, teeth, and clothing. Wear plain clothes if need be, but *don't* wear soiled or ragged ones. And don't ever put a pin where a hook or button ought to be. No man can continue to love a woman who is slatternly.

Third, allow at least an hour *every* day for reading and meditating on new thought lines, *and for going into the silence. Let nothing rob you of this hour, for of it will come wisdom, love and power to meet the work and trials of all other hours. Remember the parable of the ten virgins and take this hour for filling your lamp, that you be ready for the Unexpected. Only in such hours can you lay up love, wisdom and power which will enable you to make the best of the other hours. Let not outward things rob you of your source of power.*

Fourth, unless you wish to fall behind the world's procession see that you spend some time every day in reading the best magazines and newspapers, taking pains to skip most of the criminal news. Read optimistically and cultivate a quick eye for all the good things. Take the *best* magazines even if you have to leave feathers off your hat and desserts off your table. If you can find an *interesting* literary club it might be well to join it and do your part of the work. But see that you do not *rob* the Peter of your energies to pay the Paul of club ambitions.

And fifthly comes your housework. This is the juggernaut department which grinds many a woman to skin and bones—and her husband discards the remains! When it comes to housekeeping a woman has need of all the love, wisdom and power she can muster in her hours of silence. Even a five room flat or cottage is more than one woman can keep *spotless* and allow time for anything else. Many things *must* be left undone. The wise woman simplifies to the last degree compatible with comfort. Useless bric-a-brac is dispensed with. "Not how much but *how good*," is her rule when buying. A few good things *kept in place*, are better than a clutter of flimsy things which pander only to an uncultured esthetic taste—and make work. *Order* is the wise woman's first law in housekeeping; cleanliness her second, which is like unto the first in importance. She lets extra rooms, furniture and fallals go *until she can pay well to have them cared for*. The same rule obtains in her kitchen and her personal dress.

The wise woman thinks of comfort and allows time for the *joys* of life, wherefore *all* her life is a pleasure.

The foolish woman is ground under the wheels of routine. To her, housework is a stern "duty" which comes *first*, and to which body, mind, personal appearance, happiness, the joy of living, all must be sacrificed.

Lastly, firstly, and all the time, the wise woman is guided in what to do and in what to leave undone, by the Spirit of Love; whilst the foolish woman is guided by the Spirit of Appearances.

Note the order in which I have written these needs of life; an exact reversal of the usual order. Housework *last*, and the Spirit of Comfort first. The tendency of every woman is to lose *herself* in troubling over the many things of her household. If she would be happy, useful, young and growing she *must* turn her life the other side up.

The best way to begin, the only successful way so far as I know, is by *Making* time for the hour of reading and meditation and silence. She must *take* the time, by sheer force of will—take it until it grows into a habit which *takes her.* Out of this hour will come first peace and self-control; and gradually she will find unfolding out of this peace and control, the wisdom to know what to do, and how; and what *not* to do. From this unfolding comes the *only* power which can make new thought practical to the individual case.

Are you satisfied with yourself and your condition? Then pursue your old ways.

Are you dissatisfied with yourself and surroundings? *In order to change them* you *must change—that which was first with you must become last* and the last must be first.

Be still and know the I *am* God of you; and, lo, all *things* shall be added. But the *things* must be last, not first.

Seek ye *first* the kingdom of Good in yourself, *and to be right with it*; and all things shall be added. All things shall be added to *you*, not to *other things*.

Be still until you find yourself—your wise, loving, joy-giving Self which dwells in the silence and is able to do whatsoever you desire.

Chapter VI: Marriage Contracts

"That article of yours, 'So Near and Yet So Far,' has worried me to an extent I am ashamed of. To my 'judgment' that article is disingenuous. It is not so much that you jumped on that poor soul with hob-nailed shoes, but that you formulated the 'jump' quite as the husband might have done. That is, if *she* would repent and change her course, she would soon find that *he* was all right, and—inferentially—all the trouble was of her making. Not one word on the other side! You even quote your own experience *against* her. My dear, *did* you really find that your 'trouble' was of your own making, and *did* you really change *anything* except your own amount of distress during the process of disintegration? Marriage is the only contract which society does not promptly admit to be broken when either party refuses to fulfill his obligations—as agreed to. And in view of the custom of ages, and the instinct in woman formed by such custom (when instinct makes the establishing of Individuality the *very* hardest thing in life for a generous woman), I think that your implication against the woman, trying with all the light she's *got* to keep her side of that very one-sided contract is simply—cruel! I wish I could get at that girl and tell her that her *only* chance for happiness is through the paradox 'Whoso *will* not lose his life *cannot* find it.' Whoso will not 'let go' of the love which his five per cent judgment claims as his only *righteous* chance, cannot inherit that which the ninety-five per cent would attract if the five per cent were 'offered up' to the spirit. This is the first time I have ever disagreed with your point of view." Jane.

That article, "So Near and Yet So Far," has brought forth volumes of comment, most of it highly favorable, and nearly all of it from women themselves. But among the writers were three critics, and among the critics one of the brightest women I know, whose letter appears above.

And she says that article is to her disingenuous. Of course it is, for she has not yet arrived at the point of *giving up her own way*. She is still a Pharisee of the Pharisees—on the surface. She is proud; she *knows* she has done her best to bring things right—according to her judgment of right; and she *does hate* to acknowledge her foolishness! She will "hold fast her own integrity" as long as there is a shred of it left! Don't I know? Didn't I do exactly the same thing? Of course. But the pressure of the great spirit of love, wisdom, justice, was too much for me; I *had* to give up my judgment; I *had* to acknowledge that there *must* be the same spirit expressing in my husband's judgment; I *had* to let go, be still and get at *his* point of view. Jane, too, will have to do it. And the fact that that article "worried her to an extent she is ashamed of," is the proof. When Truth presses her point we worry until we can hold out no longer; then we give in.

One of the other two critics writes that over that article she "shed the first tears in over seven years." Then she asks me if I don't think I was a "little hard on the Taurus woman," and goes on to reveal plainly that her tears were those of *self-pity*. Don't I know? Haven't I shed quarts of such tears? Of course. But not more than an ounce or two were shed after I gave up my own way. But this second critic is arriving just as I did, and as Jane will—arriving all unconsciously to herself. Her letter sounds like a chapter from my own thinking of a dozen years ago. She gives a bird's eye view of her husband—no, of her husband's *faults*; she tells how she reads new thought literature on the sly—just as I did; and she winds up with this *piece* of good advice:

"I will say to such, live your own life as God intended you to, regardless of the fact of your husband. Be brave, hope, will and pray. Dress, look sweet. If your husband tells you he doesn't care how you look but to not come near him with your foolishness, as mine does, why, let him live his life in his own way, make home attractive for your own sake, read good books; and in time books will be your chum."

The third critic, too, is full of self-pity, though she does not mention her tears; and her letter is a long portrait of her husband's faults. She wants a little encouragement to leave him, but she is afraid he will go to the dogs if she does. So, like a generous woman, she sticks to him and makes the best (?) of a bad bargain.

Jane says my article was "cruel." Dearie, it was—as the surgeon's knife is cruel. But it is the truth, and it hurts but to make way for healing. The woman who blames has in her eye something worse than a cataract. The woman who sheds tears over her "fate" is moved by the "meanest of emotions." She attracts "cruelty," not only from that article, *but from her husband.*

It takes *two* to quarrel, *and either one can stop it.* It takes *two* to maintain "strained relations," and *either one can ease the strain.* The principles I tried to elucidate in that article are as applicable to a man as to a woman. But it was a woman, a Taurus woman, who asked me; therefore I talked straight to her. And *I* am a Taurus woman who has been through the same mill; and I wrote not from a hardened heart but from one made tender by experience and the Spirit of Truth. My point of view "might have been the husband's" *if* the husband had been an unusually just one. And I must say the husband's point of view is more apt to be *just,* than the wife's; for the reason that a woman is more apt to be blinded by *emotional self-interest.* In proportion as man or woman is ruled by emotion his judgment is distorted. *As a rule man's judgment* is straighter than a woman's. But judgment is a shallow thing, based upon *already revealed facts.* Woman's intuition goes to the heart of things and flashes facts into revelation. Women as a rule *see farther*, but are apt to misjudge what is *close at hand.* Only as man wakes in woman and woman in man do right judgment and love commune. Why not judge with the husband, as I *feel* with the wife? Is any man *totally* depraved?

Jane feels abused because she thinks *I* think that in family strains the woman is more at fault. *In a sense* I do. *Women cannot only make and unmake empires but they* do *make or fail to make harmonyat home.* Why, men with all their power are mere rag babies in the hands of women of *tact.* Women are the *real* power in the world—the power behind the throne. If only they would develop that particular kind of power instead of coming around in front of the throne to lay down the law!—instead of measuring their *man*-strength against man. Real *woman*-strength will move the most stubborn of men. If I "blame" the woman *(I blame neither, any more than I blame a child for childishness)* it is because *I know she is the ruling power.* Her responsibility is determined by her real power.

And above all a Taurus woman may rule her home—*and does.* Either she rules by force—for she has more than her share of the man in her—and makes war and trouble for herself and others; or she learns her lesson and rules by *loving tact*; in which case her husband rises up and calls her *blessed.*

The *woman who knows and rules herself* is the woman of Proverbs XXXI, 10th to 31st verses. Her husband is honored among men *because he is honored at home*; and because he is honored he *lives up to it*. Why, girls, you hold your husband's destiny in the hollow of your hand, in a far greater sense than any man holds a woman's.

But as I said before, *it takes two to make an unhappy home and either one can bring harmony out of discord*. Any ordinary woman can do it *if she will*. And any extraordinary man can do it quite as well as an ordinary woman.

This is not a question of what "society" admits; it is a personal question between one man and one woman. It *is* a partnership, whether society so admits or not. And the failure of one of the partners to live up to the expressed or implied agreement does not justify the other party in the misdoing of her part *as long as they live together*. Does one theft or murder justify another? No! Neither does a neglectful husband justify a scolding or spiteful wife, nor *vice versa*.

Two people marry *first*, for the happiness of love; and second, for home privileges. No matter whether love flees or not, *as long as they keep up* the home-privileges partnership it should be done in the spirit of harmony. Remember, it takes *two* to destroy harmony and *either one can restore it*. If marriage is not a love contract let it at least be a harmonious business contract. If you can't, or won't, *adjust yourself* to your husband, then leave him. Don't stay and half-do your part of the business and cultivate hate and contempt. It's hell. *Get out*.

I have known several couples who lived years in comparative happiness after love had flown; who were kind to each other, considerate, business-like. The wives made pleasant homes and the husbands came and went at will. In their spare time the wives developed their personal interests and "lived their own lives," as critic number two advises. When the husbands took cranky streaks the wives simply made light of it to themselves, and forgot it as soon as possible. They lived on as comfortable terms as if the wives were simply *first-class* hired house-keepers; little crankisms were all in the bargain. Eventually every one of these couples separated, and nearly all the parties are now *happily* married. *And every couple parted amicably*; each being *satisfied* to terminate the old partnership.

To me a divorce is not a disgrace, but a family row *is*. And I suspect that most divorce *rows* are worked up to *drown guilty consciences*. Neither has done his best by the other, and he knows it; so he raises a great row to fix attention on the other's shortcomings that his own may escape observation.

Until a man and woman have succeeded in living up to their home privileges in a manner befitting honest and intelligent man and woman, *they can't be sure that they are not fitted for a real loving union*. Friction over small things obscures vision and judgment, and hate hides the lovableness that *must* lie in every being. Get rid of the rowing over little things of every day life, and you will be able to love as much as your marriage will permit; *and you will be free to dissolve the entire partnership if you desire*.

Did I *really* change anything? *Yes*. Is it "anything" to bring peace and quiet pleasure and comfort and appreciation where their opposites were wont to hold bacchanale? *Yes*.

No woman who *honestly* tries the course I have endeavored to outline will ever doubt that she really accomplishes *something*; neither will she regret.

Here is a word every married woman will do well to heed as long as she lives with her husband: *If you can't have your way without a fuss, then try his with a good will.*

Peace be unto you; peace, which is the foundation for *all you desire.*

Chapter VII: Some Hints and a Kick

"And now, Elizabeth, let me suggest something. Punch up the *men* a little in the matter of cultivating cleanly habits, etc. Women are preached to eternally on these matters and the men wholly neglected. It would be a 'new thought' to take to the men a little and might assist in making more of them fit companions for the sweet and cleanly women they delight in associating with. The absolute neglect of the masculine sex by writers on these subjects causes them to think that nothing in the way of the aesthetic is expected of them. It is a wrong to the men not to en-me and make me his chum as well as his wife. Help courage them to aspire to a common plane with woman in the matters of purity and cleanliness. Cleanliness is next to Godliness, but no more so in the case of woman than of man. It is time for equality to be recognized in this matter as in all others." Carrie.

It is funny how many women squirm when reminded that it is they who set the pace in the home! We are always longing for power and a field of effort, and then when a 20th century prophetess arises and tells us we *are* all but almighty, and shows us how to direct our almightiness to accomplish results, we—well, we squirm. One would think some of us are a little bit ashamed of the pace we have been setting, of the things we have been accomplishing with our almightiness! You know, our first impulse when we see an error in our own selves is to sound the trumpet and charge upon the error in the other fellow. Is this why Carrie wants the men scolded?

Well, *don't* they get scolded? What are their wives and daughters and sweethearts for but to scold 'em or coax 'em into cleaner ways of living? No use to talk to men as a class, about anything but politics. Don't you know that Adam couldn't even taste an apple until Eve coaxed him? Adam is a great theorizer; he will gaze at an apple and tell you that he ought not to eat it, and *why* not; he will even amble long and wishfully about that apple; but it takes *Eve* to wake in him the *living impulse* to take it. Just so with matters of personal neatness. He knows—oh, yes, knowing is his long suit!—he knows he "ought" to be neat; and he thinks he wants to be; but unless Eve and the serpent come along he hasn't the *living impulse*.

And Eve must not lose sight of the serpent, however far away the dove may fly. Eve must use wisdom and tact, as well as example; if she would have Adam accept her standard of cleanliness she must see to it that her example is *beautifully* clean instead of *painfully* so. There are men who are careless about their persons simply as a matter of relief from the painful cleanness of their surroundings.

Then there are Adams who are careless for lack of interest in pleasing Eve. In these cases you will find that Eve has little or no interest in pleasing Adam; or that she overdoes the matter of trying to please, and frequently dissolves in tears and precipitates countless reproaches upon luckless Adam.

Then there are Adams who are careless from petty spite—with shame I say it. And with greater shame I say, you will find their Eves are spiteful, too; probably more spiteful than the Adams; for Eve, you know, is generally smart enough and ambitious enough to outdo Adam in any line of endeavor—especially in the use or misuse of the tongue.

In matters of niceness it is Eve who sets the pace. Adam is built for strength; Eve for beauty and adornment. It is *natural* for Eve to set the pace and for Adam to follow, in all matters of detail and niceness. Whether Adam follows with good grace or ill depends upon Eve and the serpent. If Eve is wise as the serpent in her, and harmless as the dove in her, she can lead Adam a *willing* captive to heaven or hell.

Now will you rise again and—squirm—because I attribute to Eve all power over Adam? Will you say I excuse Adam's transgressions and come down hard on Eve? I suppose so. But the very fact that you resent the imputation is proof that in your heart of hearts you know I have hit *very close* to the mark. When an arrow flies wide we are merely amused at the poor marksmanship; but the closer the arrow strikes to the center the more excited we grow—either with resentment or admiration, according to our sympathies.

In matters of cleanliness, niceness and adornment Eve sets the pace; and if her pace is a graceful one and *not too fast* Adam follows. In due time he *acquires the habit* of doing the little ablutions and adornings Eve has taught him.

If your Adam is *very* careless about these matters you may depend upon it that when he was growing up his mother was either dead or careless or tactless; and you may safely suspect that Adam in his previous state of existence was a forlorn old bach. So be gentle with him, for it will take time to correct the faults of such an Adam.

But don't give up, Eve, dear. Be gentle, but be firm and persistent. Use your ingenuity in finding ways to make Adam *want* to please you; and if you can look back over a year or two and see that he *has* improved in *some* respects at least, that there are even one or two little tricks of niceness which have become almost if not quite habitual, then hold a little praise meeting and rejoice. Praise him for learning, and praise yourself for what you have succeeded in teaching him. And if your success has come *without friction*, if you have inspired Adam to *want* to please you, then glorify yourself exceedingly—*all to yourself, of course*. If you let Adam know you are managing him even for his own good, he will show his independence by going back to his old tricks—just as *you* would do if in his place. If there has been friction, or lack of success, let it wake you up to use henceforth *more of the wisdom and love which is in you*.

Now this little homily is written ostensibly to women; but all my men subscribers will read it and applaud. *I wonder how many of them will see that every word of it is as applicable to themselves, as to their mothers, sisters, sweethearts, wives?* Every Eve is Adam at heart, and every Adam is Eve; and what in sauce for Adam will prove equally effective with Eve. Adam and Eve are both green, and growing. They are the two halves of a ripening peach, brought together by the Law of Attraction or Love because at this stage in their development *they fit*. You will be inclined to doubt that every Adam's nature fits his Eve's, but I say unto you judge not according to outward appearance but judge righteous judgment. Now listen:—Every human being has his manifested good points and his *latent* good points. The manifest good points of a man are the Adam of him; the *latent* good points—the weak places in him—are the Eve of him—the interior as-yet-undeveloped part of him. The strong points, the good points, of a woman are the Eve; the weak points, where she is as yet undeveloped, are the Adam or interior nature of her.

If it were not for personal attractions, particularly the attractions of one man and one woman, the *latent* parts of both men and women would remain forever undeveloped and their strong points would continue to grow stronger. In time (supposing the race did not die out), there would be two classes of people utterly different and at variance with each other—two opposites with no understanding or sympathy for each other.

Attraction brings together opposites; the strong, steady man falls in love with a frivolous butterfly; a handsome woman attracts a homely man and *vice versa*; a strong, capable woman marries a sickly, incompetent man—and supports him; a sentimental woman is attracted to a matter-of-fact man who develops her common sense by pruning her sentimentalities; an artistic temperament is drawn to a phlegmatic; a sanguine to a bilious; a mental to a vital; an active man marries a lazy wife, or *vice versa*; a bright man marries a stupid girl; and so on and on.

Man and wife are a rounded whole in which the man manifests what is latent in the woman, and the woman supplies that which in the man is as yet undeveloped. Just as Eve coaxes, or scolds, Adam into habits of neatness; as Adam coaxes, scolds or drives Eve into having his meals on time, thus developing her self-command and *promptness*; so they act and re-act upon each other to develop a thousand latencies of which they, and the onlookers, are more or less unconscious.

The foolish Adams and Eves fret and strain against these processes of development, and bewail their "mistake" in marrying; not seeing that the association is really benefiting both. The wise Adams and Eves reduce the friction *by kindness*, by *co-operation with each other*; Adam *tries* to please Eve, Eve tries to please Adam, and both are kind about it, wherefore in due time their *appreciation* for each other grows, and mayhap their love grows with it. If love wanes instead of growing at least they are *friends*, and can *part* as friends if they so desire.

Someone has well said that without a model husband there can be no model wife. I believe it. As long as man and woman are held together by love, attraction, or "conditions" (in its last analysis it is *all* the Law of Attraction, or *God*) they are literally *one*, no matter how hard they kick against the oneness; and neither man nor woman can *alone* be a model, any more than one side of a peach can be *entirely* ripe and sweet and the other side entirely hard and green.

So when I speak to Eve about tact and kindness I speak to *the Eve in Adam* as well as in Eve herself.

And what I say of the attractions of man and wife applies equally well to other family relationships, to friendships, to acquaintanceships and even to our relationship to the people we pass on the street or *the heathen we never saw*. Every person who touches us even in the slightest degree, *is drawn by the law of attraction because we need him to bring out some latency in ourselves, and because* he *needs us to help develop some latency in him*. It is our own highest desires (the god in us) which constitute the attraction.

"Oh, but *that* can't be," you exclaim, "because So-and-So brings out only the *evil* in me. He makes me feel *so* hateful and mean." Let us see, dearie. *The hateful and mean feelings are due to your* resisting *that which his influence would bring out of you*. For instance, you were late at your appointment with him. Of course you *thought* you had a good excuse; but if promptitude were *one of your strong points*, instead of one of your latencies, you would have been on time in spite of that excuse—if it were your *habit* to be on time you'd have swept aside a much greater hindrance before you would have allowed yourself to be behind time. Now So-and-so is naturally prompt and, having had some experience with you he knew you were not; so when, he having arrived fifteen minutes ahead of time as it is *his* nature to do, *you* came tripping in fifteen minutes late—smiling confidingly as you excused yourself (he, having spent the half hour in cultivating a grouch at you for not being as prompt as himself)—he, of course, looked sulky and answered shortly. Then you pouted and finally *worked yourself* into quite a temper over his inconsiderateness and crankiness because of that paltry little fifteen minutes he had to wait. He *worked himself* into a temper because you were not on time; you *worked yourself* into a temper because he wasn't "nice." All that working was your individual doings.

But it all resulted in your resolving that if ever you had another engagement with that man (you'd take good care not to if you could help it, though!) you'd be *on time* if it killed you. Of course you didn't tell him so. And *he* resolved that the next time he made an engagement with you he'd know it, but *if* he did he would make up his mind to be *on* time instead of ahead of time, and he'd not care if you *were* late.

So you see, the Law of Attraction accomplished its divine purpose in attracting you two to make that engagement—it waked in you a *resolution* toward promptness; and it waked in him a *resolution* to be *on* time rather than *before* time in future, and to be civil if you happened to be late—since you are only a woman and can't be expected to appreciate the value of promptness!

This is the way all our associations in life work together for good *to develop our latencies*, to strengthen our weak points. *The wiser we are the less emotion we waste in resenting the developing process—the more readily we see the point and take the resolution hinted at.* You see you and your friend had had other such experiences as the one described—you had been late before when So-and-so condoned the matter and said nothing. *He let you off so easily that you never thought of resolving not to be late again.* You *felt* that he had been displeased but you depended upon your niceness to make it all right again, and it never occurred to you to call yourself to account and *resolve* that it should not happen so again. You were *too heedless* to take a hint, so you had to have a kick.

You may set this down as a rule without exceptions: *That all the kicks you get from relatives or friends come after you have ignored repeated hints from your own inner consciousness and them.* You have gone on excusing yourself *without correcting the fault* (perhaps without seeing it) until the Law of Attraction stopped hinting and administered a kick. And if *one* kick will not cause you to develop that weak point the Law of Attraction will bring you other and yet harder kicks on the same line. *You will attract* worse experiences of the same sort.

It is this very law which makes married folks (or other relatives or friends) quarrel. Adam refuses Eve's *hints* about neatness, and Eve kicks—harder and harder. Eve refuses Adam's hints and he gets to kicking. *It* always *takes two to start the kicking,* and either one can stop it. *A frank acknowledgement of error and a* resolution *to mend your end of the fault no matter what is done with the other end; then a pleasant expression and* no more words;—this will stop the kicking. *And in proportion as you learn to take the* hints *you attract, you will cease to attract kicks.*

By all of which I am reminded of that old testament statement that *'the Lord hardened the heart of Pharoah.'* The "Lord" or "Lord God" of the old testament is what I call the *God in us*, or the Law of Attraction in us; and the "God" of the Bible is The Whole—the God *over all* as well as *in the individual.* It is the *God in us* which attracts to us our experiences, *in order to teach us wisdom and knowledge.* Pharoah was not *wise* enough to let those people go, so the God in Moses gave him a hint—which he failed to take. Wherefore he attracted a gentle kick in the way of a plague. This dashed his ardor a bit and he gave permission for the Israelites to go; but he was only *scared* into doing it; and after the plague was called off he was not wise enough to keep his word—here was a great lot of valuable slaves which he *could* keep, and why shouldn't he?—his word was easy broken and all's fair in business; so *his heart hardened* and he held the Israelites. So he attracted a harder kick; which failed to accomplish its purpose. Kick after kick came, each a bit harder than the last; each scaring Pharoah for the moment, but *none convincing him.* He still thought it *right* to hang onto his slaves if he could, and he had the courage of his convictions. A man of such splendid courage seems worthy of a better fate. Pharoah had the courage of a Christ, coupled with the ethics of a savage, whose only law is his own desire of possession. Because he could not take the hint and *see his mistake,* he attracted a series of kicks increasing in power until one finally landed him in the Red Sea. Perhaps a glimmer of the truth reached him as the waters rolled over. But his soul goes marching on and his mistakes are still re-incarnating here on earth.

Is Adam kicking, Eve? Take a hint before he kicks harder. Is Eve making things warm for you, Adam? Take care you jump not out of the frying pan into the fire. Are circumstances plaguing you, Everybody? Take the hint lest worse plagues arrive; learn wisdom and avoid the Red Sea.

Be not wise in thine own conceits. *Lean* not upon thine own understanding, but in *all* thy ways *and thy neighbor's ways,* acknowledge that the One Good Spirit leads, and He shall direct thy feet in paths of peace and pleasantness.

The proof of foolishness is unrest and friction.

The proof of wisdom is peace.

Be still and know the Lord thy God, and learn from what He draws to thee.

Chapter VIII: The Heart of Woman

"My wife has fallen in love with another man. She keeps house for me and I am trying to show her all the love I can but it seems to have no effect upon her. I love her dearly and desire to win her back. What should be my attitude toward her and toward the man?" A.J. (who is one of many who have thus written me.)

Goodness knows! *Be* good and you will know. In other words, be just to all three before you are generous to anybody. Of course that is not easy to do, but it is possible; and it is the only thing you can never be sorry for afterward.

First, get down to first principles. There are three *individuals* concerned—three separate and complete beings, each with his inherent right of choice. Nobody *owns* anybody else; nobody "owes" anybody else anything in the way of "duty." Each individual stands on his or her own two feet and makes an effort at least to go where he or she will find the most happiness.

Every one of these three Individuals has made mistakes—he or she has thought happiness was to be found in this place, or that. He or she has made the choice and trotted on his or her two feet to this place or that, only to find happiness was not there as he or she supposed. *We don't always know what is for our happiness.* But goodness knows!—and *all* our mistakes work together for ultimate happiness.

In the truest sense there are *no* mistakes; a mistake being simply a case where things failed to come out as we calculated. *They came out right nevertheless.* That is, they came out right for our enlightenment. By them we grew in wisdom and knowledge. Next time our judgment will be better.

The wife in this case no doubt thinks just now that her marriage to A.J., was "all a terrible mistake." If so she is making another "mistake." That is, she is thinking what "ain't so." Whatever experiences she has had with A.J. were drawn to her by herself, for her own enlightenment and development. They were all *good*.

It *may* be that she and A.J. have gained from their association all there is in it. Doubtless the wife thinks a separation and a new marriage would make her supremely happy. May be it would. May be her judgment is right this time.

On the other hand it may be wrong, as it has been oft before. Many a woman has jumped out of the frying pan of one marriage into the fire of another.

Only time will tell. If this new love is the "soul mate" she thinks, the attraction will be all the stronger and steadier in a year or two from now. If he is not the soul mate she thinks him, the attraction will wane.

I know women who, under similar conditions, have elected to wait; women whose consciences would not allow them to leave a kind husband or young children for the sake of gratifying their passion for another man. I have known these same women to despise a year or two later, the men they had thought themselves passionately and everlastingly in love with. They have never got over thanking whatever gods there be that they were saved from that rash step. I have known *many* cases of this kind, and have received many letters of fervent thanks from both men and women who followed my private counsel to *let time prove the new attraction* before severing old ties and making new ones.

And I must say that *not one* who waited but has said to me, "I am *glad* I waited"; *whilst many who did not wait have bitterly regretted.*

A love affair is emotional insanity. Lovers are insane; not in fit condition to decide their own actions. The state of "falling in love" is moon-madness. For the time being the lover's sense of justice, his reason, his judgment, is distorted by *reflections from another personality.* This is especially so in the woman's case, for the reason that she is generally a creature of untrained impulse, instead of reasoning will.

There is that recent case of the beautiful and beloved Princess Louise who ran away from her royal husband. She thought she loved Monsieur Giron so devotedly that she could bear anything for the sake of being with him. And surely she was miserable enough in her old environment. But when it came to the reality she could not bear the consequences. She wanted her children; her proud spirit winced at the snubs she got; she longed a little for the old life; and familiarity with her soul mate revealed the knowledge that he was not *all* soul. She flunked miserably and went home to her sick child. You see, she was literally love-*sick.* Her mind was disordered; a life spent with her soul mate loomed to her so large and dazzling that all other things were as nothing. She couldn't for the time being see straight. She was literally insane.

If she had only *waited* until the new wore off her passion! Waited until she saw things in their proper proportions and relations to each other; until she was *sure* she could *live the life* made inevitable by her change.

That is the trouble;—love-sick-ness *blinds her to the truth.* When she wakes up by *experience of the truth, she wishes she hadn't.*

The only safe thing for a woman to do who finds herself married to one man and in love with another is to *wait*, a year, or two or three years, until time proves her love and *she knows in her heart* that she can make the change and never regret it, no matter what happens. *You see, she can* never *be happy with the new love as long as* conscience or heart *reproaches her for her treatment of the old love.* It behooves her to consider well.

Time will prove the new love. In many such cases times reveals the idol's feet of clay. He shows that his love is for *himself*, not for her. He pouts and kicks and teases like a petulant child. He wants her *now*, no matter how she may suffer in consequence of his haste.

In spite of herself, in spite of her love for the new love, she finds he is not panning out as she supposed. She begins to see his other, his everyday side—the side she will have to live with *if she goes to him.*

Now is the husband's chance. She *knows his* every-day side, from experience; she has tried it in weal and woe. If he rises to this occasion the Ideal Man, he stands a fair chance of winning from his wife a *deeper* love than she has yet given any man. He may catch her *whole* heart in its rebound from the idol with feet of clay.

To a husband in such a position I would say, *Be kind.* "There is nothing so kingly as kindness!"—and true kindness under this most trying condition will in time win even a recalcitrant wife's admiration and love—*if the two are really mates.* If they are not real mates; if they have outgrown their usefulness to each other; the sooner they part the better. To hold them together would only be another "mistake."

Because a man and wife were mates five or ten years ago is no proof that they are mates today. We are all *growing*, and it is often literally true that we "grow away" from people.

Every loved one who goes out of our lives makes room for a better, fuller love—unless we shut ourselves in with our "grief."

It is said that Robert Louis Stevenson fell in love with the wife of his best friend. He told his friend frankly, intending to leave the city. His friend questioned the wife and found she reciprocated Stevenson's love. Stevenson stayed with his friend in Paris and the wife went to her father's home in California. A year later, the attachment between his wife and Stevenson still remaining, the friend applied for a divorce. Then he and Stevenson journeyed all the way to California together, where Stevenson was married to the ex-wife. The ex-husband attended the wedding, and that same evening announced his engagement to a girl friend of Mrs. Stevenson.

I glory in the friendship of those two men who refused to allow the unreasoning caprices of love to sever their love for each other. A separation and remarriage like that is a *credit* to all parties concerned. *It is the quarrels and estrangements which are the real disgrace* in cases of separation and remarriage.

John Ruskin was another man too great and too good to resent love's going where it is sent. He had married, knowing that her respect and admiration but not her *love*, were his, a beautiful and brilliant girl much younger than himself. They lived happily a number of years. Then Ruskin brought home the painter, Millais, to make a picture of his wife. Artist and model fell in love. Ruskin found it out, and refused to allow his wife to sacrifice herself for him. He divorced her and gave her to Millais, and the three were life-long friends.

If I were a man in such a case as A. J.'s I should treat my wife as I would a daughter. I would treat her as an Individual with the right of choice.

Many a daughter has rushed headlong into a marriage which her relatives opposed and she regretted at leisure.

If someone grabs you by the arm and pulls hard in one direction you are forced to pull hard in the opposite direction, or lose your balance and fall. If a daughter is pulled away from the man to whom she is attracted, her Individuality rebels and she pulls toward him harder than she would if let alone. She *chooses* to follow the attraction which at the time is pleasanter than that between herself and her frowning relatives.

Remembering this I would *free* daughter or wife and trust to the God in her to work out her highest good. I would *believe* that whatever she chose to do was really for her highest good. If I *really* loved *her* I would *prefer* her happiness to my own.

And in it all I should be *deeply* conscious that whatever is, is best, and that *all things worked together for* my *best good as well as for hers.*

Whatever appearances may show to the shortsighted, the real *truth* is this:—*Justice reigns; the happiness of one person is not bought at the expense of another; the law of attraction brings us our own and holds to us our own in spite of all its efforts to get away; it never leaves us until,* through some change or lack of change in ourselves, *it has ceased to be our own.*

A man's "mental attitude" toward the other man in such cases as A.J.'s should be the same as toward other men—the attitude of real kindness toward an Individual who, like the rest of us, is being "as good as he knows how to be and as bad as he dare be."

This does not mean that the husband shall allow himself to be used for a door mat, nor held up for the ridicule of the neighbors. A sensible father expects his daughter to observe the proprieties. The daughter of a sensible father is more than willing to meet these expectations. In the same way a sensible husband will expect his wife to see no more of the lover than "society" permits her to see of any man not related to her. No sensible American woman will jeopardize her good name under such circumstances. She will control her feelings until she has proved her new attraction and been duly released from the old. If a woman will not conduct herself in a self-respecting manner the sooner she leaves the better for the husband. As for herself, she will learn by experience—as Princess Louise did.

Love is the mightiest force in creation. It will not be gainsaid. But it can be controlled. To pen it up too completely brings explosion, devastation. To give it too free rein means madness with no less devastation. To *direct* it within reasonable limits is the only safe way.

It takes a cool head and steadfast heart to meet such emergencies as A.J.'s. And eye hath not seen nor ear heard the "Well done" and its attendant glory, which enters into the heart and character of the man who meets such condition and conquers—*himself*. Not once in a thousand lives has a man such opportunity to prove his godship and bless himself and the world.

Chapter IX: The Law of Individuality

All growth is by *learning*.

All learning comes by the gratification of desire. Truly, experience is not only the best teacher, but the *only* infallible one.

The gratification of desire, good or bad, leaves always one imperishable residue of wisdom. The rest of the experience goes with the chaff for burning.

Desire points invariably according to the individual's intelligence. In proportion as this is faulty his desires are "bad."

What *is* a bad desire, anyway? In the main "bad" desires are self-made or thoughtlessly accepted. Dancing is wicked to a Methodist and "good" to an Episcopalian.

But aside from these personal standpoints which are legion there is an immutable Law, to which intelligence is conforming all action and thought—the Law of Individuality—the Law recognized and expressed by Confucius and Jesus in negative and positive forms of the "golden rule"; "Do not unto others what ye would not they should do unto you."

Interference with the freedom of the individual is "bad"—that is, *it invariably brings pain* to the one who interferes, in thought or deed. Listen to this:

"You cannot know anything of the sources or causes of the crisis you are judging, for no one who knows will tell you, and you would not know if you were told. The depths of elemental immortality, of self-deceit and revenge, lie in our eagerness to judge one another, and to force one another under the yoke of our judgments. When there is the faith of the Son of man in the world, life will be left to make its own judgments. The only judgment we have a right to make upon one another is the free and truthful living of our own lives." George D. Herron.

This forcing of others, in mind or action, under the yoke of *our* judgment is the only possible way we can break a *real* Law. To be *ourselves* and to leave others free is to "*be good*." Dancing will come and go, and come again; so will fashions of all kinds; conventionalities and creeds; but this Law remains an eternal chalk line to be toed. And eternal torments await him who does not toe it.

Take the case of a man who desires to "run away" with another man's wife. The one immutable Law of Individuality says *no man owns a wife*. Instead of this being a problem with two men and one man's property as factors, it is a case of *three individuals* with god-given rights of individual choice. You have heard it said that "*where two are agreed* as touching anything it shall be done unto them." It takes two to make, or to keep made, a bargain. No matter what hallucinations in regard to ownership any man may labor under, *he does not* own a wife. He has no more "rights" over one woman than over another, or over another man, except as the *woman herself gives* him the right and *keeps on* giving it to him.

The Law of Individuality is absolute, and in due time husbands will know better than to imagine they own wives; wives will know better than to be owned; and the other man will not imagine he can gain great pleasure from "running away" with anything. Each will be free and leave the others so.

But "as a man thinketh in his heart so is he." Until a man *recognizes* the Law of Individuality his actions are governed by the Law he *does* recognize, and his desires act accordingly. When he desires to "run away" with anything his *conscience* tells him he is stealing. If desire is strong enough he steals a wife, and eventually suffers for it. For, though he may not have broken a real law, he *has* broken an imagined one and in his *own mind* he deserves punishment and in his own mind he gets it. "As a man thinketh so *is* he," and what he is *determines what he attracts*.

Never was a deeper, truer saying than Paul's "*Blessed is the man that doubteth not* in that thing which he alloweth." The man who *waits*, until he is "*fully persuaded* in his own mind" will be blessed in following desire, and he will grow in wisdom thereby.

The man who *thinks* his desire is "bad" and yet follows it, will grow in wisdom *by the scourging he gets*. He has transgressed *his conception* of the One Law and suffers in getting back to *at-one-ment*.

In either case he *grows in wisdom* and eventually he will desire only in accordance with the One Law of Individual Choice.

There is no question of "ought" about it. The individual is free to follow desire or to crucify it. And the fact is, *he follows desire when he crucifies it*. He *desires* to crucify desire, because he *is afraid* to gratify it.

The man who is not afraid follows desire and grows fast *in wisdom and in knowledge*. He may make mistakes and suffer all sorts of agonies as a result. But he learns from his misses as well as from his hits, and he progresses.

The man who is afraid to follow desire crucifies *his life* and stunts his growth.

It were better for the individual to follow his desire and afterward repent, than to crush his desires and repent for a lifetime under the false impression that the universe unjustly gives to another that which should have belonged to him.

There is just one kind of growth—*growth in wisdom*. We hear of children "who grow up in ignorance." We likewise hear that the earth is square and the moon a green cheese. Children can no more grow in ignorance than they can grow in a dark and air-tight case. *All* growth, mental, moral, spiritual or "physical," is by increase in in-telligence; i.e., by *recognition* of more truth. All things exist in a limitless sea of pure wisdom waiting, waiting *to be understood*. As fast as this universal wisdom is used it becomes *in-told—intelligence— recognized* wisdom. We *breathe in wisdom* and grow in intelligence. *All* growth, mineral, plant, animal, man or god, conscious or unconscious—*all* growth is by this process. It is *desire* that makes us breathe. Everything cries out for more, *more!—it* cannot define always *what* it wants, but it *wants*, with insatiable craving. It is *more wisdom* the whole creation groaneth and travaileth to get. "Give me more understanding or I die!"—the visible eternally cries out to the Invisible. Desire is the ceaseless life-urge of all things, from amoeba to archangel. Desire is "Immanuer'—*God with us—God in* us to will and to do."

Chapter X: Harmony at Home

"I have recently married for the second time. My husband is a splendid man but his grown up children are not in harmony with me. Good people, but a different point of view. I make no pretensions to perfection, of course, but I do try to do the best lean."

This is the gist of several letters I have received from as many different women. I will answer them together.

When you enter a new home the matter of importance is *not* whether your new relatives harmonize with you, but whether *you* harmonize with *them*. It is for *you* to do *all* the adjusting.

This may seem hard, but it is not. It is an easier matter for one person to readjust her living than for a whole family to change. The family has not only its individual customs to hold each one, but its family customs as well; whilst you have left your family and have only your individual self to readjust. If you refuse to adjust yourself, for no matter what reason, you will act upon this family you have entered, as a red hot iron would act upon a pan of water—there'll be boil and bubble, toil and trouble and the family will fly to pieces. All because you came in with *positive* notions of your own which you insist upon enforcing.

But if you come into the family like a lump of sugar into a glass of water you will all, *in time* melt together and the whole family will be the sweeter and better for your coming. Whatever there is in you which is better and sweeter than their own ideas and customs will in time be *absorbed* by the family; for what is good is ever positive to the less good, and has a power of its own to convert; and every human soul, if left free, will eventually *choose* the good.

The only danger lies in your tilting your nose at *their* ways and ideas, and insisting upon your own. That rouses the sense of *individuality* in them and they then fight for *their* ways and ideas—then there's boil and bubble and sputter and flying apart.

Learn to vibrate *with* people where you can and keep still when you can't. *Look* for the little things you can enjoy together, and make light of the others. Recognize their *right* to differ from you, and *remember* that "*all* judgment is of God"—*their* judgment as well as *yours*.

All this differing of judgment among the people of earth is simply *God reasoning out things*. All the brains God has are your brains and mine. Just as in your brain you reason things for and against, wondering which is right and waiting for time and experience to decide; so God reasons one way through *your* brain and another and opposite way through *my* brain, and then rests and observes until the "logic of events" shall show *him*, and us, the point of real harmony. Just be still and *let* God think through your brain, and don't kick up a muss because he thinks out the other side of things through my brain, or your new relatives' brains.

Toleration is a great thing; but loving *willingness* to *let* God think out *all* sides of a question through all sorts of brains, is a glorious thing. Let's stand for our point of view when it is called for, but don't let's insist upon it. Let's remember always to use God's "still, small voice."

Do I need to tell you that what I have just said applies to you whether you have just married a second time or not? The whole world is our family, you know. Let's respect it and be kind to it, and *trust* it to recognize and appropriate our point of view just as far as is good for it. Let's be more interested in getting at the *other* points of view than insisting upon our own. That is the way we shall grow in wisdom and knowledge. And, too, that is the way we shall all get close enough together to really see the truth about things.

Chapter XI: A Mystery

"I desire to come face to face with the person or persons who are controlling and influencing my husband against his home and children and myself. He has been estranged from us all for several years, although sleeping under the same roof. Once I can find out the person or cause of his actions I can remove the effect, for I shall know just what to do. I want to solve the mystery."

The chances are you will never find that out, and if you did it would do you absolutely no good. Your husband is no dumb fool to be "influenced" this way or that by two women! He is a man with ideas of his own. If he was disappointed in you as wife, he has possibly turned to some other woman. If so the more you pry and suspect and hint around, the more positively he will turn away from you. If you "found out" and made things warm for him or another he would simply hate and despise you and be the harder set against you. This is the Law.

The thing for you to do is to recognize your husband's *right* to make and answer for his own mistakes. Then drop the whole thing from your mind and calculations.

Then treat your husband as you would any man who came to visit you. Make yourself as attractive and cultured and agreeable as possible, and look out for his comfort, but never get in his way nor question his doings. Stand square up on your own feet and be as fine a woman as you know how to be—as gracious a one. If he does love some other woman it may be but a temporary infatuation and if you are attractive and kind and sensible and independent enough he may return to his first love in his own good time.

If not, why, no matter. Just you get interested in life on your own account and let him do as he will. If he does care for another woman he deserves credit for not deserting you, as many a man would have done. Just respect and honor him for the good that is in him, instead of condemning him mentally because the good does not show just according to your ideas of how it should.

Love does not stay put, no matter how hard folks try to keep it put. All we can do is to be as lovable as possible and thus do our part to *attract* love.

It may be that you are simply a sentimental goose who imagines her husband is "influenced" away from her, because, forsooth, he does not pay her the attentions he used to.

I was once that kind of a goose myself, and it widened a breach that did not then exist except in my mind; widened it until at last it became a real breach—my husband went elsewhere for his companionship. I was too morbid and finicky and exacting for a healthy man.

Just as the husband of the woman in "Confessions of a Wife," in *Century* did. I read that serial each month and feel like shaking that little simpleton!—she is just the kind of a sentimental hair-splitting little idiot that I used to be! Instead of getting at her husband's point of view and enjoying *with* him, at least sometimes, she insists on acting the martyr because he will not dawdle around and gush at her feet.

Whatever is the cause of your trouble the only cure for it is Common-Sense. Live your own life, cheerily, happily, and enter into your husband's life so far as you can. Take all the good things that come your way and rejoice in them, but don't moon around and fuss because you can't have the sort of love-life described in some sentimental novel. Your business in life is to *love*, not to *be* loved. The latter is a secondary matter and the first is the thing that brings happiness to you. Go in to win now, and you can develop within yourself the full Life that you really desire. All you desire is yours and you will realize it in due time. But every moment you set your thought on straightening out Some Other body's life you are delaying your own realization and happiness.

Chapter XII: The Family Jar

"If a man and woman love each other and are every way suited to marry should they yield to the opposition of his grown daughter?" M.A.

This question in varying forms comes to me often. It always stirs within me something I used to call "righteous indignation." And incidentally it makes me smile. Translate the question into Plain English and anybody can answer it without hesitancy. Put it this way: When two Individuals know what they want and the whole world approves, should they go away back and sit down because a third Individual tries to interfere with their inherent right to the pursuit of happiness?

Of course *not*. A man or woman old enough to have a grown daughter is old enough to know whether he wants to marry again. Not even the most precocious daughter is a better judge than her father as to what is best for his own happiness.

Ah, there's the rub! It is not *his* happiness she is concerned about. It is her own. A new marriage would interfere with the daughter's plans. She would have to give the chief place to the new wife. She would have to give up a share of the prospective inheritance she has more or less consciously been counting upon. So she opposes her father's re-marrying.

But apparently not on these grounds—dear, no! Her father is "too old," or "too weakly," or the intended wife is "not nice." The daughter conjures up a dozen excuses, but never the *real* one; of which she is not fully conscious herself,—and *doesn't want to be*.

The parent's "duty" to children is great; far greater than the child's duty to parent; but parental self-sacrifice should certainly *not* be continued for life. A grown daughter is an Individual, who should stand on her own feet and make her own happiness *without* curtailing the happiness of parents.

Let her leave her father to a renewal of youth and happiness; or let her gracefully and kindly accept her rightful second place and use her loving energies in helping to make bright the home.

A sensible, well trained, loving daughter will do one of these two things.

A sensible, well trained, loving parent will consider his daughter's feelings and will do all he can to gain her *willingness* before he marries; but he will not make a lasting sacrifice of his own and the other woman's happiness simply to please a selfish girl.

If daughter and parent are not sensible, well trained and loving, it will be a case of frying pan or fire either way.

The recognition of individual rights to the pursuit of happiness according to individual desire, is the only basis of happiness in family relations.

The daughter who *helps* her father do as he desires will find *him* ready to help *her* do as *she* desires. And *vice versa*.

The daughter who "opposes" her father's marriage is quite apt to be the daughter who has *been opposed by her father*; he reaps as he has sown. Or else she is the daughter who has been brought up with the idea that parents are a mere convenience for her use.

The way out of the Family Jar is often labyrinthine; but the Loving Individual can always thread it.

Chapter XIII: The Truth about Divorce

In January *Psychic and Occult Views and Reviews* the editor, M.T.C. Wing, presents a view of "Wives and Work" which is anything but an *occult* view of the subject. He evidently still clings to the old notion that man was made for the family, and not the family for man. He inveighs against George D. Herron and Elbert Hubbard *et al* because they permitted themselves to be separated from their wives. Apparently he thinks the chief end of man is to tote some woman around on a chip, and the fact that in his callow youth man picked out (or was picked out by) the wrong woman, cuts no figure in the matter. Man must keep on toting her even if he has to give up his life work by which he has been enabled to supply the chip, not to mention the other things the woman demands.

All of which is the very superficial view of the world at large, and has no place among new thought, "occult" teachings. It is entirely too obvious—to the old-fashioned sentimentalist, who is blind to the real facts in cases of separation.

The sentimentalist gets just two views of the family, and draws his hasty conclusions therefrom. He sees first a happy family, a charming, clinging little simpleton of a wife, with half a dozen or so infants clinging to her skirts and bosom, and her round eyes lifted in adorable helplessness to the face of that great, strong lord and master, her husband. In his second view of the family he beholds this strong man turn his back upon this adoring family and walk deliberately forth to self-gratification, leaving them to perish from hunger and grief. Fired with these pretty and entirely fanciful pictures the superficial observer burns with indignation and calls down anathema upon the head of the deserter.

The fact is that *no* man ever deserts a family under such conditions. There is always a long period of disintegration before any family goes to pieces—a period of which *both* man and wife are well aware. When a separation comes it is *really* a relief to *both* parties. The only real pain in such cases comes from the spirit of *revenge*, or a desire on the part of one or the other to pose as injured innocence, that she or he may rake in the sympathy and fire the indignation of just such uninformed friends as M.T.C. Wing.

I have known a lot of people who separated—known them intimately and observed them well. In not one of these cases did the deserted party claim to *love* the deserter. In all there was a real *relief* when it was all over. In every case the one thing which had held them together so long was *fear of disgrace*. "Oh, *what* will people think of me?"—is the first cry of everybody— especially women. It was *that* which made the deserted one unhappy and resentful. It is that which makes many women pose as injured innocents and rate the deserter as a villain. And all the time *in secret* they are glad, *glad* that they are relieved of the burden of living with an uncongenial husband or wife.

Of course there are other reasons why women hate to be left by their husbands. One is that their support is apt to go with the deserter.

Public opinion keeps many a family in the same house years after it really *knows* it is separated widely as the poles.

The dread of having to take care of herself keeps many a woman hanging like grim death to a man she knows she does not love, and who despises her.

The fear of public opinion and the love, not of money, but of *ease*, holds together under one roof tens of thousands of families who have been *occultly* and really separated for years.

A man is held by the same sentimental notion that M.T.C. Wing has—that he must "protect" the woman. So he stays in hell to do it. He *has* to stay in hell *until she gets out*.

In almost every one of these separation cases it is the woman and *not* the man, who gives the signal. In George D. Herron's case the wife offered to take a certain sum of money and release him from supporting her. He met her conditions—and bore all the odium like a man. To her credit be it said she did not pose as an injured woman. I know nothing about Elbert Hubbard's case, but I venture to say that if he and his wife are separated that *she* was the one who did the leaving act.

We hear a lot about the "Biblical reason" for divorce; but I say unto you that infidelity is no reason at all for divorce. The one just cause for separation is *incompatibility of temper*.

A man is an Individual; a woman is another Individual; and neither can make himself or herself over to please the other.

When two people from lack of similar ideals and aims cannot *pull together* the quicker they pull apart the better it will be for them—and the children, too.

I know well a couple who lived together long enough to have grown children. For nearly a score of years they pulled like a pair of balky horses—what time they were not doing the monkey and parrot act. The husband stayed out nights and tippled. The wife sat at home and felt virtuous. Finally the woman worked up spunk enough to do what she had been dying to do for years. She packed up and left. Now she is happily married to a man she can pull *with*, And he is married to another woman who pulls with him. She has quit feeling virtuous and he has quit tippling. They are both prospering financially. The children have *two* pleasant homes, and more educational and other advantages than they ever dared hope for. Everyone of the family is *glad* of that separation.

The family is an institution of man's own making. It is a good and glorious thing so long as it serves to increase the happiness and health of its members. But whenever the family institution has to be maintained at the expense of the life, liberty or happiness of its members it is time to lay that particular institution on the shelf.

What God does not hold together by *love* let not man try to paste together by law.

One great cause of the increase of divorces is the financial emancipation of woman. Women can now get out and take care of themselves, where a few years ago they had to grin and bear it; or bear it without grinning.

If the new thought means anything, Brother Wing, it means that every individual man or woman, has the *right* to life, liberty and the pursuit of happiness wherever and with whom he chooses to seek it, so long as he or she does not attempt to abridge the same rights for others. It means that a woman is as much an Individual as a man, and must stand or fall, hold her husband or lose him, *on her own merits*. The new thought deals with Individuals regardless of sex.

Marriage is a partnership, subject in the eyes of Justice to the same rules which govern other partnerships. Let us be just to the deserter, be he man or woman, before we are sentimentally generous to the deserted.

And don't let us be *too* sure that we know all the facts in these separation cases. It is human nature to fix up outward appearances for the benefit of the passer-by.

Seek rather to *understand*. Condemn not.

Has any one told you it is lucky to be married?

I hasten to inform you it is just as lucky to be divorced, and I know it.

Chapter XIV: The Old, Old Story

This is the springtime, when fancy lightly turns to thoughts of love and everybody wants to go a-soul-mating. Consequently my mail is leavened with letters from those who are unhappily married but who are sure they have got their eye on the One who from the foundation of the ion was intended for them. They all want to leave the old mis-mate and go to the new found soul mate, and they all want my advice and encouragement—to do it! Some of these writers have already left their husbands (?) and want to know whether or not they should go back, or go on. To one such I wrote the following letter, which I publish in the hope that it will help others to find and follow *themselves*. Here is the letter:

One thing at a time! Get off with the old love before you go fretting about a new one! Don't you think you are a silly girl to ask *anybody's* advice as to whether or not you are to go back to your so-called husband? If *I* know what *you* ought to do I don't see what *you* are worth to yourself or the universe. The truth is that *you* are the only person in creation who can make that decision. If you don't yet *know* that you have a right to make your own life as you see fit; if you don't yet *know* whether or not you could go back to him; then *be still* until you *do* know.

You know things today that you did not know yesterday, and tomorrow you will know things you "can't decide about" today. So attend strictly to business and keep still, and stiller yet, until you know what is best to do.

Then *do* it.

So much for the old love. As to the new one, not even *you* can know for certain whether that other man would pan out the soul mate you now imagine him. But the Law of Love, or Attraction, will *prove* whether or not he is what you think. *Your Own* will come to you, and all creation can't hinder it—*If* you keep that man was *not* what I longed for, a real comrade; sweet and cool, and free in your own mind, and make the best of *this* day as it comes along.

Ages ago I had a similar experience to yours. I found the only and original one intended for me. But I was tied to another man—*not* by a ceremony, for that ties nobody, but by my own conscience, which compelled me to "stand by" the man I thought "needed" me. So I stood, though I thought my heart was broken. In a few years I found that my soul mate was no mate at all!—I wouldn't have had him as a gracious gift! I felt like Ben Franklin who, as a barefooted boy, resolved that when he grew up and had pennies he would buy a stick of red striped peppermint candy; but when he grew up and had the pennies he didn't want the candy.

I have learned to smile at that experience as the bitterest and sweetest of my past life, and the source of volumes of wisdom. The *Law of Attraction knew* and the Law kept him from me. I afterward found the real comrade, and *more* than the joy I thought I had forever missed!

"We are pretty silly children, dearie, without the child's best quality, *trust*."

Just you *let go* of everything and everybody and apply yourself to doing *this* hour, with *love*, what your *hands* find to do; and trust the Law to bring you in due time *all* the good things you ever desired.

Accept what comes as *from* the Law; meet it kindly and do your best.

The time came when I left my husband and secured a divorce. This may be your time to leave, or it may not. But *no* one can know but yourself, and you will know as soon as you really *want* to know what is *right*, and get quiet enough to find the decision *about which you have no doubt.* "*Blessed* is he that *doubteth* not in that thing which he alloweth." "He that doubteth is *damned already.*" When you are *sure*, then go ahead; and the whole universe, seen and unseen, will work together for you and with you.

What is it that ties you to one man and not to another? Not the words of a priest or a justice of the peace. It is *your thought* about the matter, and *his* thought about the matter, which ties you. You may not have thought you were tied until the preacher told you; but not his words but *your acceptance* does the real tying.

If you are ever freed from a husband you must *think* yourself free—just as you must think yourself free from any other bondage. I thought myself free several years before I applied for a legal separation; so that when I did apply it was to me merely a technicality.

Divorce or no divorce you are *tied* to a man until you think yourself untied.

Be still and find your mental freedom. Then you will know what to do.

A year after I wrote the above letter to a young woman who wanted to leave her husband and go to her "soul mate," I received from her another letter in which she thanked me from her heart for my letter, which, she said, had saved her from a terrible mistake. She had let time try the new love; who was found sadly wanting. More than that she had come to love and respect her husband as never before. Many others, both men and women, have written me to the same effect.

Can you learn from the experiences of others—learn *caution* at least? I hope so. Be *sure* you are right before you resort to separation.

In the meantime make it the aspiration and business of your life to know *that* all *things are* now *working for good to you and your mate, and all you hold in common.*

Keep sweet, dearie, and *let* them work—at least until you know exactly *what* to do, and *how* to do it; and can feel *sure* in your heart of hearts that, *whatever the consequences*, you will never regret your action.

Printed in Great Britain
by Amazon.co.uk, Ltd.,
Marston Gate.